SUBSIDIA BIBLICA

12

subsidia biblica - 12

ALBERT VANHOYE, S.J.

Structure and Message
of the
Epistle to the Hebrews

EDITRICE PONTIFICIO ISTITUTO BIBLICO — ROMA 1989

This is a publication in one volume of two previously published booklets: 1) Albert Vanhoye, *Le Message de l'épître aux Hébreux* (Cahiers évangile, 19; Paris: Service Biblique Évangile et Vie, Éditions du Cerf, 1977), here translated in a slightly reedited form by James Swetnam, S.J. 2) Albert Vanhoye, S.J., *A Structured Translation of the Epistle to the Hebrews* (Rome: Pontifical Biblical Institute, 1964), previously translated by James Swetnam, S.J., and here presented in the same translation in a slightly reedited form.

ISBN 88-7653-571-3

Editrice Pontificia Università Gregoriana
Editrice Pontificio Istituto Biblico
Piazza della Pilotta 35 - 00187 Roma, Italia

Preface

The topic of the priesthood has been the cause of many discussions in recent years. In the New Testament the only work which treats priesthood at length is the Epistle to the Hebrews. If, then, one wishes to discover the Christian view of priesthood one must begin with this inspired text. Unfortunately Christians, even educated Christians, are not familiar with the epistle. True, it is difficult to read. But once one has entered into it, it proves fascinating.

Certain trends in contemporary Scripture study present us with a key for entering more easily into the thought world of the epistle. For one thing, there has been an ever greater interest in recent years in rhetorical analysis of the biblical writings. For another, structure is increasingly seen as important for the interpretation of a work. Each part of a text is understood only if it is viewed in the context of its relation to the whole.

A careful study of the rhetorical techniques utilized in the Epistle to the Hebrews along with a detailed analysis of its structure leads to what can only be termed a veritable rediscovery of this writing. From the vantage points thus gained one can admire the remarkable literary virtuosity of the author and the profundity of his teaching. The priesthood of Christ stands revealed as a reality at once both elevated and near. It is the basis for an unshakeable confidence and of a demanding dynamism which unites at all times the twin dimensions of filial docility towards God and brotherly solidarity with men and women.

I am indeed grateful to Fr. James H. Swetnam, S.J., editor of the series "Subsidia Biblica", for his suggestion to unite in one volume two works of mine which are mutually complementary and which present the principal results of my researches in the Epistle to the Hebrews. And I am grateful to him for having translated these two works into English. Thanks to him many English-speaking readers who have had neither the time nor the possibility to read my doctoral dissertation, published in French, can now see for themselves the most important of its contributions and verify their accuracy from the literal translation of the text of the epistle.

I am convinced that having thus studied from close at hand the Epistle to the Hebrews they also will feel a lively sense of gratitude towards the translator. Because of him they will have been helped efficaciously to appreciate the literary beauty of a masterpiece, and to discover for themselves a number of the essential aspects of the "unfathomable riches of Christ".

Rome, May 24, 1989

A. VANHOYE, S.J.

Table of Contents

CHAPTER I

Some Preliminary Points

1. "To the Hebrews" or "To Some Christians"?

Some years ago an Italian sociologist studied masculine and feminine first names among the inhabitants of the Italian city of Bologna. In reporting the results of this investigation the journalist of the Italian daily *Corriere della sera* pointed out how annoying it could be for a young woman to be tagged with a first name which seemed to be masculine, or for a young man to have a first name which seemed to be feminine. He himself was such a person and he described with no little humor the variety of vexations which he had to undergo.

In the New Testament there is an analogous situation, but one which afflicts not a person but a document. As a result of circumstances which we are ignorant of, a stirring homily on the priesthood of Christ has received as a title the words "To the Hebrews", a title which does not correspond to its contents. The normal effect of this unfortunate title is to dissuade Christians from taking any interest in this writing or at least to skew their perspectives on it from the outset.

The distorting title is a pity, for this homily is a genuine treasure. It contains inexhaustible doctrinal and spiritual riches and it presents them with a literary mastery which is extraordinary. Nor does it remain satisfied with theory, but is concerned also to urge on the Christian community to live its faith. It is remarkable also in that it gives to Christ the titles of priest and high priest, something which no other New Testament writing does. Better still, it effects a vigorous synthesis of the Christian faith and centers it on the subject of priesthood. Of all this the title "To the Hebrews" does not give the slightest hint.

We should note that the title "To the Hebrews" is not part of the text. It was prefixed to the homily without having any explicit connection with the text. In this regard there is a clear difference from the letters of St. Paul. These latter bear titles which find confirmation in the text itself. For example, the letter titled "To the Galatians" fits in well with the address "to the churches of Galatia" (Gal 1,2) and it questions the "senseless Galatians" (Gal 3,1). In contrast, in the document which we are discussing one looks in vain for a mention, even in passing, of the "Hebrews".

The Hebrews are never named in the document. Nor is the name "Jews", so frequently used by Paul, found in it, nor "Israelites", nor any reference to the "circumcision". In fact, the text contains no exact designation of the addressees. It is clearly speaking to Christians (cf. Heb 3,14), and Christians of long standing at that (cf. 5,12). But the author neither indicates the place where they live nor their ethnic background. He does not speak of what they were before their conversion. He does not make use of any distinction between Jews and pagans. The one reality which attracts his attention is their calling to be Christians: with might and main he seeks to foster this call (cf. 2,3-4; 3,1; 4,14; 10,19-25; 12,22-25; 13,7-8). In this connection he is led to ponder the problem of the relations between the Old and the New Testament. But he also feels constrained to take up a position against certain Judaizing tendencies which were making themselves felt in his day. It is doubtless this latter aspect of the document which has led to the choice of the traditional title. An unfortunate choice, we insist, for it does not correspond to the essential orientation of the work, which is to deepen faith in Christ and give new impulse to Christian life. Rather than the title "To the Hebrews", it would be more precise to put "To some Christians"!

2. A Letter or a Sermon?

In speaking of "To the Hebrews" the custom ordinarily is to fill out the traditional title by adding the word "epistle" — "Epistle to the Hebrews". Or one says "Letter to the Hebrews" to make the document more lifelike. This is another misunderstanding. "To the Hebrews" is not a letter but a sermon, at the end of which has been copied out a note as an appendix, drawn up when the text of the sermon was sent to a distant community. The note contains only a few brief verses. It consists of the last four verses of the present text (13,22-25), to which one must add on a brief sentence (13,19) inserted immediately preceding the solemn conclusion of the sermon (13,20-21). The tone of these verses (13,19.22-25), at once simple and friendly, marks them out clearly from the sermon as a whole which has been composed, as we shall see, according to all the rules of the art of oratory.

Were it enough to change the literary genre of a work to add on at the end three sentences of greeting, the designation "*Letter* to the Hebrews" could be justified. But how can one maintain such a position? Let us suppose that Bossuet had sent to a friend a copy of his "Funeral Oration for Henrietta of England", writing on the final page "Give this discourse a good hearing. I am coming soon.

Receive my greetings". Would it follow that this masterpiece of the art of speechcraft should then be included among examples of letter-writing, alongside the letters of Madame de Sévigné? Obviously not. "The Letter" to the Hebrews is simply not a letter. From the beginning (1,1) to the end (13,20-21) it belongs to the genre of preaching. In fact, it is the only example which we have in the New Testament of the text of a sermon which has been preserved in its entirety. In other instances there is always question either of bits of preaching incorporated into letters or of literary compositions worked into narrative texts.

In our Bibles the Christian sermon with the title "To the Hebrews" is included among the Pauline letters, for the tradition of the Eastern Church attributes it to St. Paul. As a matter of fact there is more than one point of contact with the great apostle. But it is more appropriate to speak here of a Pauline origin in a wide sense, as Origen already was doing in the third century. "To the Hebrews" was not written by St. Paul. The personality of its author, such as is manifested in its vocabulary, its style, its trend of thought, is clearly different.

Excursus: Who Is the Author of Hebrews?

A. Is the Apostle Paul the Author of Hebrews?

Is the Apostle Paul the author of Hebrews? No, for Hebrews reveals a different personality.

Paul	The Author of Hebrews
a. A vehement, irregular style	a. A style which is always well turned and serene
b. Likes strong contrasts	b. Relishes smooth transitions
c. Often projects himself into his work	c. Stays in the background
d. Defends his apostolic authority: Gal 1,1.12; 2 Cor 11	d. Does not claim to be an apostle: Heb 2,3
e. Often says "in Christ", "Christ Jesus", "Jesus Christ Our Lord" or "Our Lord Jesus Christ"	e. Never uses these expressions, but prefers original formulations to prepare the way for the name "Jesus": Heb 2,9; 3,1; 4,14; 6,20; 7,22; 12,2.24
f. In citing the Old Testament often says "Scripture" or "it is written"	f. Never uses these expressions but usually writes simply "says"
g. Never speaks of "priest" or "high priest" or "priesthood"	g. Speaks constantly of "priest", "high priest", and "priesthood"

N.B.: These observations hold for the sermon (Heb 1,1 – 13,21) and not for the final note (Heb 13,19.22-25); this latter may well be from the hand of the apostle Paul.

B. *Does the Author Have Some Connection with Paul the Apostle?*

There is a close connection in important matters between the author of Hebrews and Paul the apostle.

a. Strong argumentation against the Law:

Gal 2,16-21; 3,19-25	Heb 7,12.16.18-19.28
Rom 4,14-15; 5,20; 8,3	10,1.8-9; 13,9-10

b. Insistence on the redemptive obedience of Christ:

Rom 5,19; Phil 2,8	Heb 5,8-10; 10,9-10

c. Manner of expressing the divine glory of Christ:

Col 1,15-17	Heb 1,2-3
Phil 2,9; Eph 1,21	Heb 1,4
Col 2,15; Eph 1,21	Heb 1,4-14
1 Cor 15,27; Eph 1,22	Heb 2,8
1 Cor 15,25	Heb 10,13

d. The teaching of Hebrews on the sacrifice of Christ (9,14; 10,10.12; 13,12) finds its best preparation in Eph 5,2.25 (cf. Gal 2,20).

e. 65 words in the New Testament are found only in Hebrews and St. Paul: for example, "struggle", "pride", "profession of faith", etc.

f. The final note in Hebrews names Timothy (13,23); there is probably question here of Paul's companion (1 Thes 1,1, etc.)

g. The final note of Hebrews ends with a salutation typically Pauline (13,25; cf. 1 Thes 5,28; Col 4,18; Titus 3,15).

C. *Some of the Many Possible Candidates*

Some ancient witnesses, more often than not hesitatingly, attribute the editing of Hebrews either to the evangelist Luke or to Barnabas, one of the early Christians (Acts 4,36) and later a companion of Paul (Acts 9,27; 11,22-30; 13–15; Gal 2), or to Clement of Rome (Phil 4,3?). Each of these candidacies has been advocated in modern times, especially that of Barnabas. But none of them has gained general acceptance.

In place of the above, people have suggested the name of Silvanus or Silas (Acts 15,22), companion of Paul (Acts 15,40 – 18,5; 1 Thes 1,1; 2 Thes 1,1; 2 Cor 1,19) and secretary of Peter (1 Pet 5,12), or even the name of the apostle Peter himself. Also suggested have been Jude, brother of James, from whom there is a brief epistle, or Philip, "one of the Seven" (Acts 6,5; 8; 21,8), or Priscilla, wife of Aquila (Rom 16,3-5; Acts 18), or Apollos (1 Cor 1,12; 3,4-6.22; 16,12; Titus 3,13), or Aristion, who according to Papias, was a disciple of the Lord. Quite recently someone has even suggested that the doctrine of Hebrews comes from Mary, the mother of Jesus.

In other words, the identification of the author is a problem! The description which Luke gives of Apollos in Acts 18,24-28 corresponds rather well with the idea which one can piece together of the author of Hebrews by reading his work: Jewish origin, education in a large Hellenistic city such as Alexandria, profound knowledge of the Old Testament, a gift for preaching, a Pauline Christian. But this is not enough to show that Apollos is really the author of Hebrews, for these characteristics could be found among other apostolic authors of the period. One has to be resigned then to uncertainty.

Nor do we know the date when the priestly sermon was composed, nor the places where it was first given and to which it was sent. Opinions vary considerably in the matter. A date shortly before 70, the year of the fall of Jerusalem and the destruction of the Temple, seems the most likely. In fact, the author describes the liturgy of the Temple as being contemporary (10,1-3.11), while at the same time affirming that it is destined to disappear (9,10).

---

3. The Priestly Sermon

All things considered it would be better as a matter of principle to change the name "Epistle to the Hebrews" because the present title keeps giving rise to confusion. As one professor aptly put it, one can make three statements about the "Letter of St. Paul to the Hebrews": 1) it is not a letter; 2) it is not by St. Paul; 3) it is not addressed to the Hebrews. It would be better called "Preaching on the Priesthood of Christ" or, more briefly, "The Priestly Sermon", as one says "The Priestly Prayer" of Chapter 17 of St. John's Gospel.

But it is difficult enough for a person to bring about a change of his surname or first name once it has been duly registered with civil authority; it is more difficult still to effect a change in the case of a writing whose title is rooted in the usage of almost twenty centuries. We have to be resigned to the *status quo*. "Epistle to the Hebrews" will remain the official title of the priestly sermon and we will continue even to speak of the "letter" to the Hebrews to make the title come alive! The only change which we could hope to make — and one which I strongly recommend to the reader — is a change in interpretation. The expression "Epistle to the Hebrews" should no longer be understood as a meaningful title but as a proper noun without meaning. I hasten to explain myself: when a word is used as a proper noun for a person, for example the name "Mr. Smith", one does not pay any attention to the sense; the only value is one of "referring" to the person so named. Mr. Smith probably has no connection with forges or metals — never had and never will. But this does not mean that he cannot be called "Smith" in a useful way. In like manner, the "Epistle to the Hebrews" becomes for us simply a proper noun, the conventional way of referring to one of the writings of the New Testament which in no way defines its literary genre or its contents. In order to facilitate this change in interpretation we shall generally shorten the tag and in place of speaking of "The Epistle to the Hebrews" we shall say simply "Hebrews". For us "Hebrews" is the proper name of a writing which we know, a writing which is neither a letter nor addressed to any Hebrews but which is a splendid example of a sermon addressed to some Christians of the first century.

Once these false perspectives have been removed we can set out with renewed resolve on the investigation of this inspired writing.

CHAPTER II

The Problem of Priesthood

1. Introduction

The remarkable originality of the author of Hebrews is shown by the fact that he is the only author in the entire New Testament to have affirmed explicitly the Priesthood of Christ. St. Paul, as we have said, never touches on this subject: not once does he speak of priest, high priest, or priesthood. When the gospels use the titles "priest" and "high priest" it is always to indicate the priests and high priests of the Jews, never Jesus. The situation is the same in the Acts of the Apostles, where the title "priest" is also used once with regard to a pagan priest (Acts 14,13). The author of Hebrews, in contrast, does not hesitate to call Jesus "priest" and "high priest". He invites his listeners to "consider the apostle and high priest of our profession of faith, Jesus" (Heb 3,1; cf. 4,14.15; 5,10; 6,20; etc.) and he affirms explicitly that the priesthood of Christ is the "main point" of his teaching (8,1).

Such a contrast is enough to give us pause. How can a point of doctrine neglected by St. Paul and the evangelists be presented as a "main point" in another inspired writing? How explain this long initial period of omission and then such insistence on the innovation?

If we wish to understand the progress of the first Christians in this matter we must first of all try to discover their points of departure, and this in turn entails that we set aside for a time our present understanding of the words "priest" and "priesthood". The effort we make will also be useful in that it will help us clarify our own ideas. It will help us to extricate ourselves from all too frequent confusions and to grasp better the differences which exist between the priesthood of Christ and the priesthoods of old.

2. The Priesthoods of Old

When one speaks of priests and priesthood, a Catholic instinctively thinks of the priests in his or her parish and of their ministry. Further, we know that all Christians share in a certain way in priesthood, and that the Second Vatican Council has reminded us of this. Finally, we know that Christ possesses the perfection of priesthood and that there is a votive Mass "of Christ the sovereign priest". It is difficult for us to discover that our way of thinking on all these points is quite foreign to that of the first Christians.

The early Christians, when they heard of priest and priesthood, thought spontaneously of the Jewish priests and of the animal sacrifices in the Temple of Jerusalem. They could also think of pagan priests and of the animals sacrificed to idols in the temples. It never occurred to them to place in the same category the Lord Jesus, or the apostles of Jesus. What leapt before their eyes was above all the differences.

A) Priesthood and Interpersonal Relations

The prerogatives of Jewish priests were varied. One could make what seems to us a bizarre list of such prerogatives, which would go from ritual sacrifices (Lev 1–9; 16) to supervision of health (Lev 13–14), while touching on casting lots (Deut 33,8; 1 Sam 14,36-42; 23,9-12; etc.), certain juridical prerogatives (for example, Num 5,11-31), the teaching about divine decisions (Deut 33,9-10; 31,9-26) and the granting of benedictions (Num 6,22-27; Sir 45,15). Further, these prerogatives took different forms in the course of centuries.

But if, beyond this diversity, we seek to find the underlying theme of the Old Testament priesthood as an institution, we find that it consists of relations between persons. In a way far superior to Greek philosophy, biblical revelation makes one aware of the basic importance for human existence of interpersonal relations. This fits in well with an important sector of modern thought and of some anthropological disciplines which stress this point. The human person never exists in isolation. An infant develops as a human person only through a network of relations with other persons. It is in meeting another person that one truly becomes alive and grows. The progressive conquest of the external world is made possible only through the creation of a great variety of interpersonal relations.

Now among relations which make up the human person there is one which is fundamental, even if we are not clearly aware of it. Other relations affect only this or that sector of existence and are found at various levels. This relation exists at the deepest level of being and is all-encompassing in extent. It conditions all other relations. It is our relationship to God. The human person is a being called to enter into relationship with God and nothing is more important for him or her than the response which he or she gives to this call. In their effort to arrive at an existence truly human, men and women have recognized, since time immemorial, this essential aspect of their human predicament.

In the face of this realization three attitudes are possible. The first is completely negative: it is a refusal to recognize the religious dimension of human existence, a refusal which in its most radical manifestation takes the form of a denial of God's existence (cf. Ps 14,1; Rom 1,21). It seems to be a simple solution, but it ends up in devastation without end (cf. Rom 1,18-32).

The second attitude seems positive but is really another kind of denial. It is religious individualism. In theory it is open to the divine, but in practice it attempts to keep the relationship with God within the limits of the individual's psychological life and to prevent such a relationship from running over into other sectors of existence. This attitude is inconsistent (cf. 1 John 4,20). To be authentic, our relationship to God must be accepted as fundamental; it is the relation that supports and guides all other relations, it is the relation whose influence is decisive at all levels of existence.

It is necessary, then, to find a third solution which avoids both "the drama of atheistic humanism" and a stifling religious individualism, a solution which corresponds fully to the call to men and women to open the entire gamut of human existence to a life-giving relation with God. This is the need which the institution of the priesthood wishes to meet. The priest is in effect a man who bears the community's responsibility of relating to God. He is called to serve the group as a whole (and consequently each member of the group) regarding everything which touches relationship with God. In other words, he is a mediator.

B) Priesthood and Ritual Worship

Ancient peoples in general and the people of Israel in particular grasped well the difficulties involved in serving as mediator. They were acutely aware of the enormous distance which separates humans from God. How could a weak and miserable being communicate with the Three Times Holy, the "devouring fire" (Deut 4,24; Heb 12,29)? When God makes himself known man feels himself gripped by fear (cf. Isa 6,5; Exod 20,18-19). The splendor of the divine light is too bright for his weak eyes; God's unlimited generosity represents for him unbearable demands. Between the onrush of God's life and the fragility of his own existence he perceives an appalling difference in density and he recognizes that a relationship with God is not possible for him without a radical transformation of his whole being, a transformation which he sees as a passage from the level of the profane to the level of the sacred. God is holy; to enter unscathed into a relation with him a preliminary condition must be met: to be impregnated with holiness through some kind of "consecration".

The solution proposed by the old cult to meet this need was a ritual solution. It consisted in a system of ritual separations.

Israel does not have the holiness needed to approach God. If it tried to do so it would perish (cf. Exod 19,12; 33,3). A tribe is therefore set apart for consecration to the service of God. And within this tribe a family is set apart for a special consecration: from this family will be taken the priest charged with maintaining good relations between the people and God. The priest is separated from the sphere of the profane by means of a consecration which removes him to the sphere of the holy. This consecration is described in detail in the books of Exodus and Leviticus (Exod 29; Lev 9): ritual bath to purify from profane contacts, anointing which imbues with holiness, special vestments which indicate insertion into the world of the holy, sacrifices of consecration. The "holiness" thus granted must be studiously maintained: rigid rules oblige the priest to avoid everything which could lead him back to the level of the profane (Lev 21). If he violates these rules it will no longer be possible for him to approach God.

Moreover, the priest's meeting with God is subject to still other conditions. One does not encounter God just anywhere, but only in a holy place. Here again there is question of separation. A holy space is a space reserved for the cult; it is forbidden to the public. To enter into a holy place the priest must conform to a ritual which calls for him to carry out in a sacred period of time sacred ceremonies, of which the most meaningful is the "sacrifice".

Here again we must attempt to free ourselves from the meaning which we ordinarily give to the words. For us "sacrifice" means "privation". The ancient meaning of the word is quite different. It indicates not a privation but a transformation. To "sacri-fice" means to "make holy", just as "puri-fy" means to "make pure" and "paci-fy" means to "make peaceful". Sacrifice is a ritual act which makes an offering pass from the profane world to the world of the sacred.

Why must the priest offer sacrifices? Because it is impossible for him unaided to pass fully into the world of God. Despite the ceremonies of his consecration he remains tied to the earth. It is necessary then to choose another living creature which can bring about this transition. The ritual orders him to choose this or that animal and to make sure that it is without blemish. This animal will be entirely removed from the profane world for it will be immolated and offered on the altar of the temple. Consumed by the fire, it will ascend to heaven in smoke (cf. Gen 8,20-21; Lev 1,1.17; etc.) or, to use another symbol, its blood will be, as it were, cast up to the throne of God (Lev 16,14.15).

This is the high point of the whole work of mediation such as the Old Testament conceived it. There is question, as is clear, of a consecration always more absolute, which is achieved by means of a series of ritual separations in stages. The priest is separated from the people in order to be set aside for the cult; he leaves profane space in order to enter into the holy place; he abandons profane activities in order to accomplish sacred ceremonies; his sacrificial offerings bring about separation from earthly life in order to go up to God.

After this ascending movement of successive separations one obviously hopes for a descending movement of divine favors. If the sacrifice is worthy of God the victim will be accepted. The priest who offers it will now be able to enter into contact with God and he will see that his prayers have been heard. Thanks to his mediation the people represented by him before God will be found in good standing with the Divinity and will obtain the graces desired: a) pardon of faults and the end of the calamities which result from them; b) divine instructions which make it possible to find the right way through the bewildering circumstances of existence; c) divine blessings, that is the application to all aspects of existence of the saving influence which a positive relation with God brings about.

Thus one ends up with the following diagram in which all the prerogatives of the priesthood find their place and take their sense:

Diagram of Old Testament priestly mediation:

2. Central component

The priest is admitted into
God's dwelling.

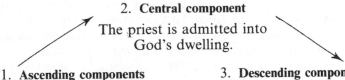

1. **Ascending components**	3. **Descending components**
An ascending series of ritual separations of which the summit is the offering to God, by the priest, of an immolated animal.	The priest hands on to the people the gifts of God (pardon, instructions, blessings).

The proper functioning of this operation obviously depends entirely on its ascending phase. Everything rests, then, on the system of ritual separations which we have indicated. This is why the Jews attached to these separations the greatest importance. Infractions of this system were punished by death (cf. Num 1,51; 3,10.38; Acts 21,27-31).

3. Jesus and the Priesthood of Old

Between the institution of the priesthood of old such as we have just described it and the human existence of Jesus, what connections could the first Christians find? At first glance, none. Jesus did not belong to this institution; his ministry was not a part of it and his death took him even farther from it.

a) As regards the person of Jesus many questions had been raised. Questions about his identity had been asked and a variety of answers given, both favorable and hostile: "he is a prophet", "a possessed person", "the Messiah", "a seducer". It is significant that no one had ever thought of calling him a priest. Yet there is nothing remarkable in this. It was all too clear that Jesus was not a priest according to the Jewish Law. For he did not belong to a family of priests or of high priests, not even to the tribe set aside for service and worship. In the ascending series of ritual separations he stood at the lowest level, that of the people.

b) Jesus never laid claim to the functions of Jewish priest. His ministry was never priestly in the Old Testament sense of the word. His work continued rather the line of the prophets, who proclaimed the word of God and announced the approaching intervention of God. One must note in this regard that between the preaching of the prophets and the ancient priesthood as institution there was often manifest a strong tension. The danger inherent in the institutionalized priesthood was to encourage the belief that an external carrying out of rite and a respecting of the necessary separations was sufficient to establish a right relationship with God. The prophets rose up against this formalism and demanded a genuine docility towards God in day-to-day existence, particularly in social and political life. Jesus clearly allied himself with this prophetic tradition. The gospels witness to the systematic battle he constantly waged against the ritualistic view of religion. They indicate that he attributed little importance to preoccupations involving ritual purity (Matt 9,10-13; 15,1-20 and parallels); he refused to give an absolute value to the sacred rest of the Sabbath (Matt 12,1-13; John 5,16-18; 9,16). He rejected the ancient way of understanding sanctification. In Matthew's Gospel Jesus twice confronts his foes with the word of God proclaimed by the prophet Hosea; "It is mercy that I want and not sacrifice" (Hos 6,6; Matt 9,13; 12,7). He thus takes a stand against the system of ritual separations whose high point, as we have seen, was the offering of "sacrifice", and he chose the contrary course of action, that which seeks to honor God in spreading the mercy which comes from him. In place of a sanctification obtained through separating oneself from others he proposes a sanctification obtained through accepting them. Preoccupation with ritual purity is abolished and is replaced with a dynamic of reconciliation and communion. Instead of multiplying barriers it is better to eliminate them.

c) The ministry of Jesus had taken on a course in the opposite direction from that of the Old Testament priesthood. But did he not turn around to join them in the end? In his death was Jesus not united to the priesthood? Is not the death of the Christ a priestly offering, a "sacrifice"? We are accustomed to give an affirmative answer to these questions and we are not wrong. But perhaps we are not aware of the complexity of the situation. To avoid being simplistic the affirmative response should come at the end of a series of reflections which begin with a negative position. It is necessary to begin by recognizing that the death of Jesus was not a sacrifice in the old sense of the term, i.e., a ritualistic sense. According to the old view, the sacrifice did not consist in the putting to death of a victim, still less in the victim's sufferings, but in the rites of offering carried out in the holy place. Now the death of Christ did not take place in the holy place and it had nothing in common with a liturgical ceremony. The death of Jesus was all the opposite: the execution of a condemned man. Between the execution of a condemned man and the carrying out of a ritual sacrifice the Israelites — and therefore the first Christians as well — saw a contrast that was total. The rites of sacrifice made up a solemn act which glorified and sanctified, an act which united to God and was the source of blessings. The death undergone by a condemned man appeared on the contrary not only as the worst of punishments but also as an "execration", the contrary of a "consecration". Cut off from the people of God (cf. Num 15,30), the condemned man was cursed and a source of malediction (Deut 21,23; Gal 3,13). In the case of Jesus the condemnation was blatantly unjust and what happened took from within a completely different meaning. But for all that it did not become ritual and did not constitute a "sacrifice" in the ancient sense of the word. It was rather, on Jesus' part, an act of "mercy" carried to the extreme; Jesus had gone to the point of "giving his life in ransom for the many" (Mark 10,45). He had died "for our sins" (1 Cor 15,3; Rom 5,6-8). This act of mercy corresponded to God's desire of "mercy and not sacrifice" (Matt 9,13; cf. Mark 12,33).

Far from closing the distance between Jesus and the ancient priesthood, the event on Calvary had increased it even more.

All this evidence answers one of the questions asked: it makes us understand why, in the early Church, no one thought of giving to Christ the titles of priest or of high priest, or of attributing priesthood to him. The long period of omission at the beginning is easily explained: there was nothing, either in the person of Jesus or in his ministry, much less in his death, which corresponded to the idea which people then had of priesthood.

4. The Question of the Fulfillment of the Scriptures

In the light of the foregoing we must now explain why a change eventually took place. Why did the omission of reference to Christ as priest not last indefinitely? Why has the theme of priesthood been introduced into the expression of the Christian faith? Is there question of a superfluous addition? Of a lack of fidelity to the primitive message? Or is there question of a genuine deepening of faith? There is no doubt about the reply: there is question of a genuine deepening of faith brought about by a question which had to be asked.

While it was normal at the beginning, the omission of thinking of Christ as a priest could not keep on without creating grave problems. It raised doubts which undermined the Christian faith. Was this new faith introducing a religion without priesthood? Did Christians form a community which dispensed with priests? Was such a situation admissible? A facile reply could not suffice, for such questions bear on a basic claim of the Christian faith. This faith proclaimed and still proclaims that Christ had fulfilled the Scriptures, that in him was perfectly realized the designs of God announced in the Old Testament. But how could this affirmation be upheld if the mystery of Christ was completely devoid of the priestly dimension so prominent in the Old Testament?

a) When we read the Old Testament we cannot fail to notice the importance of the institution of the priesthood. A major part of the Mosaic Law is taken up with the organization of worship and of the priesthood (Exod 25–31; 35–40; Lev 1–10; 16–17; 21–24; Num 3–4; 8; 15–19, etc.). In the historical books one notes that the influence of the high priest keeps growing. After the Exile he even ends up by becoming the only head of the nation, combining religious authority and political power (cf. Sir 50,1-4). In the 2nd century B.C. it is a family of priests who instigated and guided the uprising agains the Seleucids and the decisive ground was a priestly one: the profanation of the Temple by the pagans was intolerable; it was necessary at any price to restore the cult of the true God (1 Macc 1–2; 4,36-59). The success of the uprising brought to power this family of priests and confirmed once again the importance of the priesthood. At the time of Christ the high priest in charge remained the supreme authority of the nation; he presided over the assembly of the Sanhedrin which the Romans recognized as the local power.

b) The historical situation outlined above assuredly brought with it negative aspects. The intrigues of some of the high priests, ambitious and without scruple, gave rise to bitter protests (cf. 2 Macc 4). But the divine institution of the priesthood was never in question, for this was affirmed not only by the Mosaic Law but even by the prophets who nevertheless did not hesitate to criticize the priests and their worship (cf. Hos 5,1; 8,13; Amos 5,21-25; Mic 2,1-9; Isa 1,10-16; Jer 2,8). Jeremiah, for example, who had the audacity to foretell even the destruction of the Temple (Jer 7,12-14), also proclaimed on behalf of God that the Levitical priests would never lack successors to offer sacrifices (Jer 33,18). And Ben Sira insistently kept issuing reminders that the priesthood of Aaron was guaranteed by an eternal covenant (Sir 45,7.15.24-25).

As a result of all this, when the fulfillment of God's plan promised for the age of the Messiah was brought up, renewal of the priesthood was included (Mal 3,3). Many Jewish writings of the 1st century B.C. witness that Israel during this period expected a priest to come in the final times. The manuscripts of Qumran in particular have many texts which speak clearly in this sense. This expectation was normal, because any fulfillment worthy of the name could not possibly set aside any of the essential elements of God's design. And priestly mediation was on all evidence one of these essential elements.

c) Thus a question arose for Christians from the very fact that they claimed to have found in Christ the perfect fulfillment of God's design. This question was as important as it was unavoidable: did or did not the fulfillment realized in Christ include a priestly dimension?

If the reply to this question was negative, the Christian position ran a serious risk of being untenable. But in view of all that has been said above, how could an affirmative reply be given? Was not such a reply impossible, given the absence of any relation — or, worse still, given the opposition — which we have noted, between the existence of Jesus and the Old Testament priesthood? And would not any attempt to innovate on this point have presented serious dangers for the Christian faith, which could have ended up being distorted?

A solid wall in front, a bottomless pit behind; the situation seemed to allow no way out. In reality, a solution did exist, but to find it one had to go to the root of things. This is what the author of Hebrews did, in the light of his faith.

Instead of falling back on the ritual prescriptions of the ancient cult, the author of Hebrews submitted the cult to a rigorous analysis, all the while letting himself be guided by the Bible itself. This analysis ended up by distinguishing, in the ancient cult, the fundamental idea and the concrete way in which the idea was executed. The fundamental idea was valid; of that there was no doubt. But the way it was carried out showed that it was deficient because of human frailty; the Old Testament itself bore witness to this.

The author made the same reflective effort on the mystery of Christ. Setting aside the baffling circumstances, he focused his attention on the profound reality of the events, and he discovered that Christ had made his own the basic project of the priesthood, and had brought it to a happy conclusion.

This double effort of reflection, on the ancient cult and on Christ, obviously involved a change in outlook on a number of points. The old image of priesthood had to be put aside to allow room for a conception which corresponds more closely to reality. In the process some aspects of the mystery of Christ were developed in a new way.

To be fair, one must observe that the author of Hebrews did not begin from scratch. In the gospel catechesis, in the apostolic preaching, and in the life of the Christian community various elements already existed which prepared the way. The most important was undoubtedly the words Jesus had spoken at the Last Supper over the cup of wine, words which declared the establishment of a covenant in his blood and hence which evoked a sacrifice of a covenant (Matt 26,28 and Mark 14,24; Luke 22,20 and 1 Cor 11,25). An unexpected link was thus suggested between the death of Jesus and the ritual of sacrifice carried out by Moses at Sinai (Exod 24,6-8). The Christian community met regularly to relive this "supper of the Lord" (1 Cor 11,20) and to hear again this word. One readily understands that St. Paul had had the idea to place in opposition (and thus in parallel) eucharistic communion and participation in the pagan ritual sacrifices (1 Cor 10,14-22). In addition, the date of Jesus' execution suggested another comparison indicated subtly by the Gospels and set forth with unmistakable clarity by St. Paul: "Christ our Passover has been immolated" (1 Cor 5,7). Christ is thus presented as a victim offered in sacrifice.

Later another Pauline text takes up the non-sacrificial formula of Gal 2,20: "He has loved me and has delivered himself up for me", filling out its meaning by situating it in a sacrificial context: "Christ has loved us and has delivered himself up for us as an offering and sacrifice to God" (Eph 5,2).

These indications — and one could add others — are not lacking in importance. Nevertheless, they do not constitute a sufficient reply, for they do not face clearly the question of the priesthood: did Christians have a priest or not? They did not show what changes were necessary in the understanding of priesthood and sacrifice in order to set forth the mystery of Christ. Together with the apostolic nucleus of which he was a member, the author of Hebrews undertook to deepen the study of this problem and he treated it in all its breadth. The Church has recognized that his work is a writing inspired by the Holy Spirit, Word of God addressed to the People of God and part of the New Testament.

Chapter III

The Literary Structure of Hebrews

This chapter runs the risk of appearing somewhat dry and uninteresting. But it is not difficult and a careful study of it allows us to enter into the very heart of the message of Hebrews. If you have a copy of the Bible which you can mark up, you can indicate in it the "structuralizing techniques of composition" listed on p. 20. The general structure of the epistle is outlined on pp. 40a-b, and a more detailed structured outline with translation is given on pp. 79-109.

1. The Importance of Structure for the Interpretation of Hebrews

In order to understand correctly the message which the author of Hebrews has left us it is not enough to read his sentences one after the other. One must also and above all figure out the composition of the work as a whole. In fact, each part receives its precise meaning only when it is situated in its place in the whole. Otherwise a secondary remark runs the risk of being considered something essential, while a central point passes unrecognized. If important connections are not known or poorly understood, the entire piece is disfigured. An error with regard to the literary structure is never without consequences on the interpretation of the thought. In a work as carefully crafted as Hebrews the results of such errors are serious.

Let us furnish at once two examples. Certain commentators divide Hebrews into two parts:

I.   1, 1 – 10,18:   Dogma

II. 10,19 – 13,25:   Moral

These commentators thus give the impression that the author treats faith first and then moral conduct, putting a sort of separation between the two spheres. On the one hand, theory and ideas; on the other, the duties arising from existence. But this is a false view of Hebrews, a writing which, on the contrary, constantly expresses the bond between the two aspects of the Christian message. This message is at one and the same time revelation and invitation —

revelation of the gift of God and invitation to respond to it in specific ways. Far from waiting for the middle of Chapter 10 to urge his listeners to live as Christians, the author of this priestly sermon already at the beginning of Chapter 2 makes a pressing appeal to them (2,1-4) and does not hesitate later to return to this theme (3,7 – 4,16; 5,11 – 6,20). On the other hand, in the part labeled "moral" he inserts many doctrinal reminders. In brief, from one end to the other, the composition of the work is marked by the alternation of doctrinal expositions and exhortations, which shows well just where the author is concerned to make faith enter into life and to transform life by faith.

Other commentators opt for a division into three parts:

I.   1, 1 –   4,13   The Word of God

II.   4,14 – 10,18   The priesthood of Christ

III. 10,19 – 13,25   Appeal to live as Christians

If this presentation is exact it follows that two important themes appear separated from each other: when the author treats of the Word of God he is not interested in the priesthood of Christ, and, vice-versa, when he describes Christ as priest he makes no mention of the Word of God. Is it true that the priesthood of Christ in Hebrews is defined only by its sacrificial aspect? We have noted above that the schema of the priestly mediation entails, among other aspects, that of the transmission of the Word of God; the priest communicates to the faithful the "instructions" of God. Would this aspect have disappeared in Christ's priesthood as presented by Hebrews? To answer this question, fraught with serious implications, we must study in detail the composition of the priestly sermon (Heb 1,1 – 13,21).

2. Structuralizing Techniques of Composition

For anyone with a taste for literary analysis, the study of Hebrews becomes extremely interesting, because the author is a master at writing. He has written his work with a talent without equal, making use of structuralizing techniques which came to him from his Jewish-Hellenistic education. Here is the list of the principal techniques used; identifying them allows us to uncover the structure of the priestly sermon:

Ⓐ   Announcement of the subjects to be discussed;

Ⓑ   Inclusions which indicate the boundaries of the developments;

Ⓒ   Variation of literary genre: exposition or paraenesis;

Ⓓ   Words which characterize a development;

Ⓔ   Transition by immediate repetition of an expression or of a word, which is termed a "hook word";

Ⓕ   Symmetric arrangements.

Below we shall refer to these various indications by labeling them with the circled letters used here.

At first sight this technique can seem to be complicated, but one catches on quickly, for it is more natural than one would imagine. The most important among the indications is obviously the first: the announcement of the subject **Ⓐ**. Before starting each part, the author states in a brief formula the subject which he is getting ready to develop. He also thereby indicates if the subject contains one point or several. To have an outline of the priestly sermon, then, it is enough to copy one after another the announcements of the subjects as they appear in the text.

But the catch is to recognize the announcements in the text without mistakes. Our author is not one of those preachers who makes outlines easy by stating straightforwardly at the beginning of their sermon that they will develop three points: one, two, and three. The author of Hebrews is too much an artist to use this mathematical way of proceeding. He prefers to use structuralizing techniques which are more subtle and which rely on the insight of the listeners.

The author of Hebrews does not indicate at the beginning the content of his sermon in its entirety, nor the succession of the different parts. But he does introduce at the appropriate place a topic which will be the subject of a first part. At the end of this first part he introduces the subject of the second; at the end of the second, the subject of the third, and so on. One arrives at five announcements in all, situated first at 1,4, then 2,17-18, then 5,9-10, then 10,36-39, and finally at 12,13.

Excursus: Inclusions

The structuralizing technique called the "inclusion" is used often in biblical texts. In certain instances an entire sentence is

repeated to serve as a frame. Thus Ps 8 has the sentence at the
beginning, "O God, our Lord, how great is your name over all the
earth!", and this is repeated in its entirety at v. 8 to mark the end of
the psalm. In the same way, at Matt 7,16-20 the beginning and
ending are identical: "It is by their fruits that you will know them".
More often it happens only in part (for example, Matt 19,30 and
20,16 or John 5,19 and 5,30); or the repetition is restricted to only a
few words (for example, John 2,1-2 and 2,11; John 9,1-2 and 9,41)
or even to only one word (Wis 2,17 and 2,20).

Sometimes we find entire literary developments structured
according to a whole system of inclusions. Thus we find the
following in the Book of Wisdom:

1,1   Love *justice*, you who judge the *earth*...

1,14-15 Hades does not reign on the *earth*, for *justice* is
immortal.

1,16   The ungodly call on *death*...worthy as they are to
belong to him

2,1   they said to themselves in *reasoning* falsely:

2,1   *There is no* cure for *passing over*

2,5   *There is no* return from *passing over*

2,6   ... let us *make use of* creatures ...

2,11   ... that which is weak and *useless* ...

2,12   Let us lie in wait for the *just man*

2,16   ... the final destiny of the *just man*

2,17   Let us see if his *words* are true

2,20   ... help will come to him according to his
words

2,21   Thus they *reason* and they deceive themselves ...

2,25   Through the envy of the devil *death* has come into the
world: they who *belong to him* will experience it

The same type of structure based on inclusions is found in the famous prayer to obtain wisdom (Wis 9,1-18) as analyzed by M. Gilbert (cf. *Biblica* 51 [1970] 301-331):

9,2	*by your Wisdom* you have formed *man*	9,2	*by your Wisdom* you have formed *man*		
		9,6	the children of *men* (are nothing) without *the Wisdom* which comes from *you*		
		9,7	You have chosen me as king of *your people*		
		9,12	I shall rule *your people*		
		9,13	what *man* will know the counsel of God	9,13	what *man will know* the *counsel* of God
				9,17	And your *counsel who has known* it
				9,17	unless you have given *wisdom*
9,18	from that which pleases you *men* have been taught and *by wisdom* they have been saved	9,18	from that which pleases you *men* have been taught	1,18	and by *Wisdom* they have been saved

Note that the words which serve to form the inclusion are often arranged in chiastic form (*wisdom, man–men, wisdom*). This makes the inclusion better still, with the final word taking up the initial word.

All the evidence points to the fact that Hebrews is part of this same literary tradition. In order to convince oneself of this one needs only compare the above with the inclusions found in the central part of Hebrews (see pp. 37-40).

3. **The First Announcement of Subject (1,4) and First Part (1,4 – 2,18): The Name of Christ**

The first announcement of subject ❹ is not difficult to recognize, for it comes where one expects it, that is, at the end of the exordium of the sermon (1,1-4) and the newness of the theme draws the attention of the reader. On completing the solemn sentence which introduces his sermon, the preacher has to indicate where he is going. Read the long introductory sentence which stands at the beginning of Hebrews, the sentence which traces the entire trajectory of God's intervention in human history (1,1-4). You notice, do you not, the sudden insistence of the author on the comparison between Christ and the angels (1,4), a comparison which involves especially the "Name" received by Christ? At the conclusion of his redemptive work Christ "has inherited a Name quite different from that of the angels". Thus ends the exordium of Hebrews. The author indicates in this way the subject which he wishes to develop in the first part. From the sentence which follows (1,5) the reader can see that in fact he begins a demonstration along these lines. He cites various passages of Scripture which witness to the fact that the name of Son is given to Christ and not to the angels.

This insistence on the "name" is disconcerting. It betrays a Semitic way of thinking. Instead of an "inherited name", we non-Semites tend to speak rather of a status acquired, of glory obtained. What the author wants to announce is really a doctrinal exposition on the glorification of Christ or, if one prefers, a "Christological" treatise. This will be the first part of his sermon.

How far does this part extend? There is a simply way to discover this. The author has let it be known that he is going to develop his topic by comparing Christ to the angels. In order to limit this part it is sufficient then to observe how far this comparison extends. The author speaks of angels all through Chapters 1 and 2. They are mentioned for the last time at 2,16. They then leave the scene and reappear only at the end of the sermon (12,22; 13,2). The word "angels" is used 6 times in Chapter 1 and 5 times in Chapter 2 and thus is a word which characterizes ❹ the first part of Hebrews and indicates its boundaries. The first part corresponds to the first two chapters in our editions. We must recall in this context that our division into chapters dates only from the Middle Ages, and that it is designed only for convenience in referring to the text. It does not indicate the structure of the biblical writings.

The other indicators of structure bear out the limits of the section and in addition they indicate its internal composition. This latter is made up of two paragraphs of exposition (1,5-14 and 2,5-18) which form a symmetrical frame **❻** on both sides of a brief exhortation (2,1-4) **❺**. The first paragraph evokes the position of the glorified Christ who is with God (1,5-14); the second shows his relation with men (2,5-18). Christ is Son of God and brother of men. On both scores he has "a name quite different from that of the angels" (cf. 1,4).

Already indicated by the variations in the literary genres (exposition, exhortation, exposition) **❺**, the boundary of the paragraphs is again emphasized by the verbal framework called inclusion **❸**, which consists in the repetition at the end of a point which has been developed of a word or phrase used at its beginning. The phrase which indicates the beginning of the first paragraph, "For to which one of the angels has he ever said?" (1,5) is taken up in 1,13 to indicate the end of the paragraph.

The same procedure serves also for the other paragraph of exposition. The first words of this paragraph (2,5) are repeated at 2,16 to end it: "For it is not to angels that...".

The listener who allows himself to be guided by these various indicators of structure realizes that the last mention of the angels at 2,16 brings the first part to a close. The author has made an exposition, brief but not without depth, of the mystery of Christ. He has developed his point with unusual balance: divine glorification on one side (1,5-14), solidarity with humans on the other (2,5-16). This harmonious arrangement **❻** reinforces the impression that at 2,16 one is arriving at the end of the paragraph begun at 1,5.

4. The Second Announcement of Subject (2,17-18) and the Second Part (3,1 – 5,10): Christ, High Priest Merciful and Worthy of Faith

Having reached the end of the first part in 2,16, the reader expects to find a new announcement of a subject **❶** to introduce the subject matter of the following part. And in fact the conclusion which began at 2,16 continues on to 2,17-18 with the appearance of a completely new subject. For the first time the author mentions priesthood and he applies to Christ himself the title "high priest". To this title he adds two important attributes, "merciful" and "worthy of faith", not mentioned previously. The position of the sentence — as a conclusion of a part — and the newness of the theme enable the listener to recognize once again the announcement of a subject.

If any doubts remain they are quickly eliminated by the sentence which follows, for this is an unmistakeable indication of the beginning of a new part. The change of tone conveys this **ⓒ**. The author abandons the impersonal tone of the exposition which he used in 2,5-18 and begins to question his listeners (3,1). This is the first time he addresses them in a direct fashion. Earlier he did not proceed in this way (cf. 1,1). And his phrasing is insistent; in all that follows there is no parallel: "So then, holy brethren, you who have a share in a heavenly vocation, set yourselves to consider...". Now — and this is the second remark to be made — the subject matter which he so urgently presses on his readers for their "consideration" is none other than that which he has just formulated in 2,17, the priesthood of Christ: "consider the apostle and *high priest* of our profession of faith, *Jesus*". This bears out explicitly the view that the sentence at 2,17 announced the subject matter of the part which is beginning. The solemnity of the questioning leads one to grasp that the subject matter is the main point of the sermon. The preceding part (1,5 – 2,18) served only to prepare for it.

In continuing his sentence (3,2) the author adds a qualifying note about the composition of the second part. Instead of repeating the two adjectives of 2,17, "merciful and worthy of faith", he repeats only "worthy of faith" and proceeds to comment on it by drawing a comparison between Jesus and Moses. He thus leads one to think that he is reserving for later on the explanation of the other adjective "merciful", and thus that the second part will have two sections which will treat of the two complementary aspects of priesthood. Christ is: 1) high priest worthy of faith as regards relations with God his Father; 2) high priest full of mercy towards his fellow brothers and sisters. The reader can easily ascertain that these two aspects correspond to the two expositions of the first part, Christ Son of God (1,5-14) and Christ brother of men (2,5-18), and that they define the two fundamental conditions on which priestly mediation is based.

In order to discover the limits of the first section it is enough to note at what point the author passes from the first topic — the authority which Christ has for faith — to the second, that of his priestly mercy. This point is found at 4,15. The preceding sentence (4,14) still belongs completely to the material concerning the authority of Christ (we cite it *in extenso* below), while the sentence at 4,15 speaks only of his capacity to exercise compassion: "For we do not have a high priest incapable of sympathizing...".

It is easy to verify the fact that from 3,1 to 4,14 there is nothing in the text which speaks of mercy. This first part is characterized by the vocabulary **❶** of faith: "worthy of faith" (3,2.5), "confession of faith" (3,1; 4,14), "faith" (4,2), "to have faith" (4,3), "a lack of faith" (3,12-19). The reader notices a variation in the literary genre **❸**, but this means only an internal division, for the subject matter does not change: there is always question of faith. After a brief exposition (3,2-6) comes a long exhortation (3,7 – 4,14). The exposition proclaims that Christ is worthy of faith; the exhortation draws the conclusion that we should give him our faith.

An inclusion **❸** noteworthy for its insight upholds the limits of the development of this section on faith. Between the initial sentence of 3,1, ("This is why, holy brothers who share in a *heavenly* vocation, you should consider the apostle and *the high priest* of our *profession of faith, Jesus*..."), and the sentence of conclusion at 4,14 ("Having then an eminent *high priest* who has gone through the *heavens, Jesus*, the son of God, let us maintain our *profession of faith*"), one notices verbal connections which are carefully wrought. According to the usual technique of the author these connections indicate that in 4,14 one has reached the end of the section which began at 3,1.

The second section begins then at 4,15. From this verse on, we find in effect all the terms of 2,17-18 dealing with the priestly mercy of Christ: to suffer, to be tested, to bring help; as well as others having the same orientation. An impressive evocation of the Passion of Christ (5,7-8) shows to what degree our high priest shared in our distress. The author places in parallel "every high priest" (5,1-4) and "Christ" (5,5-10). The arrangement of the whole **❸** leads the reader to look for the ending of the section after v. 8. And in fact one finds in 5,9-10 a solemn sentence which brings the passage to a close while broadening the perspective. This sentence refers to Christ and makes a threefold affirmation with regard to him:

(1) "made perfect";

(2) "he became for all those who obey him cause of eternal salvation";

(3) "proclaimed by God high priest in the manner of Melchizedek".

A change of literary genre **❸** and of vocabulary **❶** takes place immediately afterwards (5,11), confirming that the second section has ended and with it the entire part which began at 3,1.

5. **The Third Announcement of Subject (5,9-10) and the Third Part (5,11 – 10,39): The Unequaled Value of the Priesthood and of the Sacrifice of Christ**

The themes expressed in 5,9-10 evidently need to be explained. What is this "perfection" attributed to Christ? What is the meaning of a priesthood "after the manner of Melchizedek"? The listener is asking himself these questions and awaits the answers from the preacher. In other words, the listener spontaneously considers the sentence of 5,9-10 as an announcement of the subject for the following part **Ⓐ**. He is not mistaken and he sees his impression confirmed, for the preacher continues: "Concerning this matter we have many things to say..." (5,11).

The sentence 5,9-10 is thus presented explicitly as the announcement of the subject of a new part. This third part will be more dense than the second. The author declares openly that "the explanation will indeed be difficult" (5,11) and he rouses the listener with an uncommonly vigorous call to pay attention (5,11 – 6,20).

At the end of this preamble he does not take up the entire three-fold affirmation of the announcement of the subject (5,9-10), but only the third point: "Jesus become high priest forever according to the manner of Melchizedek" (6,20; cf. 5,10).

Thus repeated at the beginning of Chapter 7, the name of Melchizedek serves as a hook-word **Ⓔ** to achieve the transition. The section which begins at 7,1 corresponds perfectly to the third point of the announcement. One can foresee that two other sections will develop the two other points. And as a matter of fact this is what happens. Moreover, the author is careful to have each of these sections preceded by a corresponding reminder for the listener.

At the end of the development on the priesthood according to the manner of Melchizedek (7,1-28) the author of Hebrews prepares a new section by taking up the first affirmation of the announcement ("made perfect", 5,9). He states in 7,28 that the high priest constituted by the oracle of Ps 110 is the Son "made perfect". In the Greek it is the very last word of the sentence. Then he immediately begins the section announced by stating: "Now the main point of our discourse is that we have such a high priest..." (8,1). The expression "such a high priest" refers back to the immediately preceding sentence which speaks of the "Son made perfect" (7,28). The section which has beginning in 8,1 will then show in what sense and in what way Christ has reached the "perfection" which grounds and characterizes his priesthood. The section takes as its subject matter the first affirmation of the first announcement of subject at 5,9, "the main point of our discourse" (8,1).

There remains then only to develop the second affirmation, that which designates Christ as "cause of salvation" (5,9). This affirmation will supply the subject matter of the last section of the main doctrinal part. The preacher will not fail to warn his listeners, in exactly the same way used in the two preceding instances. As in 6,20 and in 7,28 he will place at the end of the section being developed a partial repetition of the announcement made in 5,9-10. In 6,20 the preamble is brought to a close with a reminder of the third point of the announcement, the priesthood according to the manner of Melchizedek. In 7,28 the section which treats this subject ends with a reminder of the first point of the announcement, the "perfection" of Christ. In 9,28 the section on the "perfection" of Christ ends with the word "salvation" which recalls the second point of the announcement, Christ the "cause of salvation" (5,9). This word, which has not been repeated since 5,9, announces the corresponding section. This section begins immediately afterwards (10,1) and proclaims the complete efficacy of the priesthood of Christ to free us from our sins (10,1-18).

The author then has developed one after another the three points which he had formulated in 5,9-10. The order of presentation has been different, however, from the order in which they were announced. The author usually explains first what he has announced last. This is what he had done in the second part: "worthy of faith" came after "merciful" in the announcement at 2,17 but was commented on before it (in 3,1-6). This is what he will do again in the fourth part, as we shall soon see. This way of proceeding has the advantage of making transitions easier.

It is not difficult to see that each of the three sections of the third part (A: 7,1-28; B: 8,1 – 9,28; C: 10,1-18) has its own distinctive features and its own well-defined limits. The composition of each section is marked by a system of inclusions ❸ worked out with great care. The reader finds not only general inclusions to mark the limits of the major developments, but also other inclusions which, so to speak, provide sets of frames within frames to set off subdivisions as well (cf. pp. 37-40). This type of composition is found elsewhere in the Bible, especially in the Book of Wisdom (cf. the excursus "Inclusions", pp. 20-22).

The patterns revealed by the inclusions show that the author does not lose the taste of symmetric arrangements ❻.

The changes in literary genre ❸ help in finding the beginning of the first section (after 6,20 one passes from the tone of exhortation to that of exposition) and the end of the third (after 10,18 one comes again to the tone of exhortation). But from 7,1 to 10,18 the genre remains unvaried and hence does not give any indication as to the internal boundaries of the sections. Other indicators amply suffice to guide us in this regard.

From one section to another the vocabulary ❶ varies in a significant way. It corresponds, of course, to the material of each section:

Section A (7,1-28) treats of the person of the priest and the position which his priesthood gives him. The glorified Christ is not a priest according to the manner of Aaron, but according to a new manner foretold in the Old Testament by the mysterious figure of Melchizedek (Ps 110,4; Gen 14,18-20).

Section B (8,1 – 9,28) considers the process which guarantees to the priest his place with God. Christ is now with God thanks to a new type of sacrifice which has conferred on him "perfection".

Section C (10,1-18) considers the results gained for the people. The sacrifice of Christ has complete efficacy for the pardoning of sins and the sanctifying of the faithful.

To put matters succinctly, these three points take up the three aspects (one could also say "the three stages") of priestly mediation such as we defined them in the outline on p. 11. The author begins with the central aspect, Section A, the position which the priest holds. Then he explains this position by the ascending dimension: Section B, sacrifice. Finally, he considers the descending aspects which come about from the worth of the sacrifice: Section C, efficacy for the people.

6. The Fourth Announcement of Subject (10,36-39) and the Fourth Part (11,1 – 12,13): Faith and Endurance

The short final sentence of section C (10,18) does not indicate the end of the entire part but only of the lengthy doctrinal exposition begun at 7,1. To this the author immediately adds a fervent exhortation which draws out the implications of this exposition for Christian living. The change in genre ❷ at 10,19 is evident. Again the preacher addresses his listeners directly by calling them "brothers" (10,19; cf. 3,1.12). He declares to them that, thanks to the blood of Jesus, they can from now on approach God in "full assurance" (10,19) and he invites them therefore to proceed apace in faith (10,22), in hope (10,23), and in love (10,24).

At 10,35 the author takes up in a final sentence the important word which had given the tone to the opening sentence of this exhortation: "full assurance". "Do not lose then, he says, your full assurance, to which is attached a great reward" (10,35). Having noticed this inclusion ❸ the perspicacious listener awaits the announcement of the subject ❶ of the following part. In effect two themes are forthwith presented. First comes the theme of the necessary endurance: "It is of endurance, in fact, that you have need..." (10,36). There follows the theme of faith which makes the just live: "My just will live by faith..." (10,38). The third part ends in this way, by announcing the fourth.

The author takes up immediately the second theme which has been announced, that of faith. The word "faith" acts as a hook-word ❺ to achieve the transition between 10,39 and 11,1. The author develops his theme by presenting the examples of the "ones of old" (11,2), that is, of the just persons of the Old Testament. In a superb fresco he praises all the achievements and all the trials of faith from Abel on to the times of the Maccabees, paying attention to Abraham, to Moses, to the Judges, to the prophets. One would have to be blind not to see the unity of this section. The word "faith" alone serves as characterizing device ❹ for it is repeated as a refrain. The author has even thought it worthwhile to add an inclusion ❸ between the beginning and the end: he takes up in the last sentence (11,39-40) the words "faith" and "to receive witness" found at the beginning (11,1-2). The literary genre ❻ is that of an enthusiastic exposition, without any explicit appeal to his listeners.

At the beginning of Chapter 12 the genre ❻ changes. The author assumes the tone of direct exhortation. The theme of endurance announced at 10,36 makes its reappearance. The listeners are invited to give evidence of endurance (12,1) after the example of Jesus who "has endured the cross" (12,2.3). That which they "endure" (12,7) is part of their education as sons of God. They would be wrong then to become discouraged. The words which characterize ❹ this development are those of endurance and of correction or of education. One finds them up to v. 11. Then comes a conclusion which encompasses vv. 12 and 13. In order to confirm that the conclusion marks the end of the section begun in 12,1 and thus also of the part on "faith and endurance", whose themes were announced together in 10,36-39, the author makes use once again of the device of inclusion ❸, but the translations do not make this evident. In the Greek text, between the phrase "let us run with endurance" of 12,1 and the phrase "make the track straight for your feet" of 12,13 the connection is close, for the words "let us run" and "track" come from the same root. It would be appropriate to translate the second "track for running" in order to make the inclusion clear.

7. The Fifth Announcement (12,13) and the Fifth Part (12,14 – 13,21): Straight Paths!

Inasmuch as verses 12 and 13 form the conclusion of the fourth part particular attention to them is in order: this is the spot where the author normally indicates what is to follow ❶. One detail can be noted with relative ease, especially if one has a good knowledge of the Old Testament. There is not only one conclusion but two. It includes two sentences: the first (12,12) corresponds to the theme of the preceding section but the second (12,13) introduces a new topic.

The exhortation of 12,12 to "set straight the slackened hands and the paralyzed knees" is taken from the prophet Isaiah (35,3). It is related to the theme of endurance as is shown by a comparison between Isa 35,3-4 and Heb 10,36-37. In contrast, the invitation of 12,13 to "make the courses straight" does not come from Isaiah: it is taken from the Book of Proverbs (4,26) and sets forth another aspect of Christian life, that which concerns behavior and not "suffering". When an introduction of a new topic takes place at the end of a part we recognize the technique of the announcement of a subject ❶! The invitation "to make courses straight" sets forth the subject of the fifth part, which will establish certain orientations of Christian life.

The first sentence of this part (12,14) specifies the direction of the "straight paths" by saying: "Pursue peace with all and sanctification...". The sentence indicates that in their activity the Christians must unite two concerns, that of harmonious relations with others and that of union with God. Christians must live the two dimensions of charity: love for God and love for others. After the fourth part, which indicated the path of faith and of hope ("endurance" is connected with hope — cf. 1 Thes 1,3 and Rom 8,25), the final part brings the perspective to completion by speaking of the life of charity. The author had already prepared us for this at 10,24-25.

A general inclusion ❷ extends from the first sentence (12,14) — "Pursue *peace*... will see *the Lord*" — to the solemn conclusion (13,20) "may the God of *peace*, who led up from the dead *the Lord*...".

Two partial inclusions mark the boundaries of two long paragraphs (12,15, "grace" and 12,28, "grace" for one part; 13,7, "leaders", "conduct", and 13,17-18, "leaders", "conduct ourselves" for the other). These long paragraphs frame another paragraph, smaller, and of a different rhythm (13,1-6), but whose composition is no less carefully crafted. The arrangement of the whole is then exactly the same as in the first part (1,5 – 2,18): two large paragraphs on either side of a short central paragraph.

The first paragraph (12,14-29) stresses above all "sanctification" (12,14), that is to say, the relation with God. It invites Christians to be worthy of their vocation. The last paragraph (13,7-18) endeavors to strengthen the cohesion of the community around its leaders, a cohesion based on the participation of everyone in the passion of Christ (13,12-13). The central paragraph (13,1-6) lays down specific orientations: lived charity, chastity, spirit of poverty and trust in the Lord. The whole of Christian life is presented as worship rendered to God (12,22-24.28; 13,15-16) in thanksgiving and real fraternal solidarity.

The solemn sentence of 13,20-21 concludes not only the final part (12,14 – 13,18) but also the priestly sermon in its totality. It gives a brief reminder of the doctrinal content (13,20) as well as of the implications for Christian life (13,21). The conclusion ends with the formula of a doxology ("to Him glory") and an "Amen". The sermon is ended. Nothing is missing.

8. A Summary View of a Masterpiece

The study which we have just concluded gives us a summary view which will help us considerably in what follows. In showing the interconnections of the text it prepares the way for our work of interpretation. But before we begin the interpretation we should pause for a moment to admire the literary perfection of the priestly sermon. For it is clear that here we have a work in which the author has invested all his ability. He did not feel that the importance of his message dispensed him from care in giving it form. On the contrary, he tried to give full force to his message by creating for it a perfect medium in structure.

a) From the very first sentence, so artistically balanced (1,1-4), one sees how the author is concerned about writing well. It is his way of showing respect for the Word of God which he has been called to transmit. Because he was endowed with a different temperament St. Paul preferred to follow other paths; he affected no small detachment with regard to "the prestige of the word" (1 Cor 2,1; cf. 1 Cor 2,4.13) and was content to pass as an "amateur in matters of eloquence" (2 Cor 11,6; cf. 2 Cor 10,10). Here is a situation where one must recognize that "each one receives from God his own gift, one this, the other that" (1 Cor 7,7) and that it would be ill-advised to impose on all a uniform way of acting (cf. 1 Pet 4,10). The author of Hebrews was a gifted writer; he did not bury his gifts but made them bear fruit for the service of Christ and the Church (cf. Matt 25,14-30).

The writer's talent is seen especially in the harmony of his composition. A taste for symmetrical arrangement is clearly one of the most obvious characteristics of the biblical literary tradition. Our author is on this point the faithful heir of this tradition. But an observation about method will be useful in this regard. In the list of indications which allow one to see the structure of Hebrews we have placed "symmetrical arrangements" at the end. This ordering is deliberate. Its aim is to alert the reader to the rather frequent methodological error which consists in beginning a study of the structure by having as an objective the discovery in the text of a symmetrical arrangement. One runs the great risk in so doing of violating the integrity of the text and of imposing on it an arbitrary arrangement of structure which is not its own.

The study of structure should, on the contrary, be undertaken with no a priori conclusions and should begin with a search for the first series of indications. These indications allow one to make out the arrangement of the text. It is only at the end, once this arrangement has been established, that one can observe if it corresponds or not to a symmetrical ordering and if it presents any noteworthy characteristics.

b) In the case of Hebrews the search for the first series of indications yields the general outline which follows:

I.		The Name of Christ	1,5 – 2,18
II.	A.	Jesus high priest worthy of faith	3,1 – 4,14
II.	B.	Jesus merciful high priest	4,15 – 5,10
		— Preliminary exhortation	5,11 – 6,20
III.	A.	High priest after the manner of Melchizedek	7,1-28
III.	B.	Made perfect	8,1 – 9,28
III.	C.	Cause of an eternal salvation	10,1 - 18
		— Final exhortation	10,19 - 39
IV.	A.	The faith of the ones of old	11,1 - 40
IV.	B.	The necessary endurance	12,1 - 13
V.		The straight paths	12,14 – 13,21

Let us recall that the grouping of the sections in five major parts is based on indications given by the author himself in his five "announcements of subject".

Now it so happens that the outline that results gives an obvious symmetry of a concentric type. By the number of their sections the five parts correspond with each other around a central part which is Number III. The First and Fifth Parts have only one section; the Second and Fourth have two; only the Third Part is composed of three sections, announced at 5,9-10, to which are affixed preliminary and concluding exhortations.

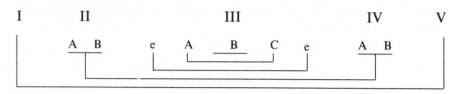

c) The length of the text in the parts which correspond to each other is exactly comparable:

i) The First Part covers 28 verses, or 32 if one includes the Introduction (1,1-4).

The Fifth Part covers 34 verses, or 36 if one includes the Conclusion (13,20-21).

In the Introduction and the First Part the grouping of verses contained in the paragraphs give the following figures: (4 vv.) + 10 vv. + 4 vv. + 14 vv. (the number in parentheses is that of the Introduction).

For the Fifth Part and the Conclusion the figures are as follows: 16 vv. + 6 vv. + 12 vv. + (2 vv.) (the figure in parentheses is that of the Conclusion).

The similarity of proportion among the units is striking. It becomes more striking still if, as is proper, one sets out the relations in following a concentric outline so that the last element of the end can be compared with the first element of the beginning and so on. Then one obtains the following correspondences:

I.   (4) + 10 + 4 + 14

and, in inverse order,

V.   (2) + 12 + 6 + 16

ii) The Second Part covers 45 verses, distributed in two sections, of 33 and 12 verses.

The Fourth Part covers 53 verses, distributed in two sections of 40 and 13 verses.

Here also the similarity of proportions is striking.

iii) The Third Part takes in 132 verses. Its preliminary exhortation (24 vv.) and its final exhortation (21 vv.) are perfectly proportioned. They frame a large exposition of 87 verses (28 + 41 + 18). This exposition is truly central, not only in the outline, but also in the bulk of the work: it is preceded by 101 verses and followed by 110 verses.

The symmetry is not only external. It affects also the subjects treated, at least up to a certain point. The most obvious instance is that of the Second and Fourth Parts. The subject matter of their two sections correspond to each other. In fact, II.A ("Jesus... worthy of faith") goes well with IV.A ("the faith of the people of old"); and II.B, which evokes the passion and the compassion of Jesus, goes well with IV.B, which insists on the need of patience in time of trial.

d) The normal effect of a concentric arrangement is to call attention to the center of the structure. This is certainly what the author of Hebrews wanted. A number of striking indications clearly show this. The central part is the most important of all. In itself it takes up more than two-fifths of the text (132 verses out of 298). The announcement of the subject (5,9-10) is immediately emphasized by the remark which develops it: "On this point we shall have much to say ..." (5,11) and by an insistent preambule (5,11 – 6,20).

In this central part (5,11 – 10,39) the section B (8,1 – 9,28) is itself central, preceded as it is by an exhortation and by a first section of exposition, and followed symmetrically by a third section of exposition and by an exhortation. The reader can see that this central section is the longest of all, not only in the central part but also in the Priestly Sermon as a whole. With its 41 verses it is longer than the First or the Fifth Part and it exceeds in length even the section on the faith of the persons of old, which contains 40 verses. Better still, it is explicitly presented in the first sentence (8,1) as the "main point of the exposition". We would do well, then, to study it in greater detail.

We have noted that this central section is itself composed according to a concentric pattern: it takes in six subordinate divisions, which are grouped two by two on either side of the center.

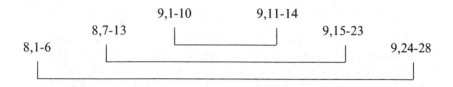

We are justified in expecting then that in the eyes of the author the subject matter of the central subordinate divisions (9,1-10 and 9,11-14) is of decisive importance. And in fact one finds there the confrontation between the old ritual cult (9,1-10) and the unique sacrifice which has been successful, that of Christ (9,11-14).

If we focus our attention on the word placed in the exact center of the entire structure (or, more exactly, on the word nearest to the center, for the center is an empty space between the two central subordinate divisions), we see that its choice has certainly not been left to chance. For this word is none other than the name itself of Christ: "Christ, he..." (in Greek, *Christos de*).

"Christ" is the first word of the positive paragraph (9,11-28). The better to place the word in evidence here the author has avoided using it in the first half of this section (8,1 – 9,10). Now, in 9,11, he insists on it and immediately joins to it the title "high priest" and describes the priestly activity which justifies the title (9,11-14).

Thus the name of *Christ high priest* has been chosen as the keystone for the entire structure. It is at the central point (9,11) of the central section (8,1 – 9,28) of the central part (5,11 – 10,39). In the general outline of Hebrews it is preceded by five and one-half sections and likewise followed by five and one-half sections. In the development of the text it is preceded by 152 verses and followed by 146 verses (without counting the five verses of the epistolary conclusion which are not part of the sermon). This is a fact of extraordinary significance. It reveals at one and the same time the unusual mastery of the author as regards literary composition and the care with which he placed his talent entirely at the service of his faith.

Excursus: Outline of the Inclusions of Part III (7,1 – 10,18)

A. *Outline of the Inclusions of Section A of Part III (7,1-28)*

(The order of words is that of the Greek text. The words placed in parentheses are words placed twice in this outline for convenience in making a point, even though they occur only once in the text.)

The general inclusion (indicated at the far right: "priest" in 7,1-3 and "high priest" at 7,26-28) take in the entire section. Two larger inclusions mark the limits of the two large paragraphs: the first (7,1-10) makes comments on the text of Gen 14,18-20 concerning Melchizedek; the second (7,11-28) makes comments on the oracle of Ps 110,4 on Christ "priest according to the manner of Melchizedek". Some minor inclusions indicate subdivisions.

The vocabulary ❿ is that of the institution of priesthood: "priestly order", "priesthood", "priest", "high priest", "Melchizedek", "Aaron", "Levi".

7,1	7,1	Melchizedek .. .. encounters	7,1	priest	7,1	(priest)
			7,3	priest	7,3	(priest)
			7,4	tithe Abraham		
			7,9	Abraham tithes		
	7,10	encounters him .. Melchizedek				
	7,11	perfection ... .. endowed by law	7,11	(perfection .. endowed by law)		
			7,19	makes perfect the law		
			7,20	oath-taking		
					7,26	high priest
7,28	7,28	... law ... . makes perfect	7,28	oath-taking	7,28	high priest

B. *Outline of the Inclusions in Section B of Part III (8,1 – 9,28)*

(See the note for the outline of the inclusions in Section A.)

The general inclusion ("to offer", 8,3 and "offered", 9,28) take in all of this section except for the introductory sentence 8,1-2. Two long inclusions define the limits of two long paragraphs. The first (8,3 – 9,10) takes a position with regard to the old worship and with regard to the covenant which is attached to it. The second (9,11-28) concerns the sacrifice of Christ and the establishment of the new covenant. Each of the two paragraphs offers at its core a development on the covenant and thus divides into three subdivisions. The section as a whole thus contains six subdivisions. These are arranged concentrically: the first (8,1-6) evokes in 8,3-5 the earthly level of the ancient cult and provides a contrast with the last (9,24-28) which affirms the heavenly and definitive level reached by Christ; the intervening subordinate divisions (8,7-13 and 9,15-23) treat of the relations between the two covenants; the central subdivisions (9,1-10 and 9,11-14) contrast the ancient ritual with the personal sacrifice of Christ.

The vocabulary ☉ is that of priestly activity and related matters: "offer" (8 times), "blood" (11 times), "sanctuary" (8 times), "tent" (8 times), "covenant" (12 times).

8,3	to offer	8,3	(to offer) gifts and sacrifices	8,2 minister
				8,6 ministry
				8,7 the first [covenant]
				8,13 the first [covenant]
				9,1 rites of worship
				9,2 fashioned
				9,6 fashioned
				9,6 worship
		9,9	gifts and sacrifices are offered	9,9 worshipper
				9,10 rites
		9,11	Christ	9,11 (Christ)
				9,14 the Christ
				9,16 neces- sity — 9,15 covenant-testament
				9,17 testator
				9,18 not without blood
				9,20 ... the blood of the covenant
				9,22 not without the effusion of blood
				9,23 necessity
				9,24 Christ
9,28	offered	9,28	Christ	9,28 (the Christ)

Excursus: The Structure of Hebrews

Exordium: The interventions of God in history: 1,1-4
➤ 1,4: **The Son is superior to the angels because**
        he has inherited a name which is much different

I. SITUATION OF CHRIST: 1,5 – 2,18

1,5-14 (exposition): Son of God superior to the angels
2,1-4   (exhortation): Need to take seriously the message
2,5-18 (exposition): Brother of men
➤ 2,17: **Become like his brothers in order to become a high**
          priest merciful (B) and worthy of faith (A) who is with God
          in order to remove the sins of the people

II. HIGH PRIEST WORTHY OF FAITH AND MERCIFUL: 3,1 – 5,10

A. WORTHY OF FAITH: 3,1 – 4,14

3,1-6 (exposition): Jesus worthy of faith, superior to Moses
3,7 – 4,14 (exhortation): We should give him our faith

B. MERCIFUL: 4,15 – 5,10

4,15-16 (exhortation): Let us go to obtain mercy
5,1-10 (exposition): He has shared our suffering
➤ 5,9-10: **Made perfect (B)**
            he became the cause of eternal salvation (C)
            proclaimed by God high priest (A)

III. UNIQUE VALUE OF THE PRIESTHOOD AND

5,11 – 6,20 (exhortation): The explanation is difficult: pay attention!

A. HIGH PRIEST according to the manner of MELCHIZEDEK 7,1-28

The biblical figure of Melchizedek announces a priesthood superior
to the levitical priesthood. Ps 110

B. MADE PERFECT

8,1-6 Ancient cult, earthly and figurative
8,7-13 First covenant, imperfect and provisional
9,1-10 Ancient institutions, powerless

CHRIST has come as HIGH

> The arrows (➤) and the letters in bold face
> indicate the announcements of the part which follows.

"Word of Farewell" (by Paul?) 13,22-25

Conclusion and doxology 13,20-21

V. THE STRAIGHT PATHS! 12,14 – 13,18

12,14-29 Sanctification (relation to God)
13,1-6   Christian attitudes
13,7-19 True community

IV. FAITH AND ENDURANCE: 11,1 – 12,13

A. FAITH OF THE ANCESTORS 11,1-40

Exposition: Faith realized and faith tested in the Old Testament

B. NECESSARY ENDURANCE 12,1-13

Exhortation: Accept testing which is necessary
for the formation of God's children

➤ 12,13 **Make the paths straight!**

OF THE SACRIFICE OF CHRIST: 5,11 – 10,39

10,19-39 Exhortation to a generous Christian life
➤ 10,36-39 **You have need of endurance (B)**
"My just one shall live by faith" (A)

C. CAUSE OF ETERNAL SALVATION: 10,1-18

As opposed to the powerless sacrifices of old the personal
offering of Christ does away with sin and makes us holy.

BY HIS SACRIFICE: 8,1 – 9,28

9,24-28 Access to heaven; true relation with God
9,15-23 The new covenant is legitimately established
9,11-14 New and efficacious institutions

PRIEST of the good things to come (9,11)

C. *Outline of the Inclusions in Section C of Part III (10,1-18)*

   (See the note for the outline of the inclusions in Section A.)

   This section is briefer and has a less diversified format. A general inclusion takes in the entire section. Other inclusions make it possible to distinguish two paragraphs (10,1-10 and 10,11-18); each of these paragraphs is comprised of two subdivisions, but the last of these subdivisions (10,15-18) does not have its limits indicated by an inclusion. The first and fourth subdivisions are related as opposites (repetition of the offerings, termination of the offerings). The second and third each express an opposition: the second, between the sacrifices of old and the offering of Christ; the third, between the priests of old, busy because powerless, and Christ, tranquil as priest because he has accomplished everything.

   The vocabulary ❿ is that of priestly efficacy: "power", "sanctify", "make perfect"; the author considers the value of "the offering" (5 times, never elsewhere in Hebrews) to do away with "sins" (9 times in 18 verses).

10,1	they offer	10,1	(they offer)	10,1	each year
				10,3	each year
				10,5	offering you have not willed, but a body
		10,10	offering	10,10	will ... (offering) of the body
		10,11	offering ... sins	10,11	(offering)
				10,14	offering
10,18	no more offering	10,18	no more offering for sin	10,18	(offering)

Excursus: A Concentric Structure in the Apocalypse

Concentric arrangements are not rare in the Bible. The easiest ones to note are those which characterize limited texts, for example, Lev 24,16-22. When longer they often lend themselves to discussion. One of the most convincing cases is that of the Letters to the Seven Churches in the Apocalypse. Let us make a rapid study of the letters following the work of N. W. Lund, *Chiasmus in the New Testament* (Chapel Hill, North Carolina, 1942). For convenience we indicate each letter by its number in the listing: 1 to Ephesus (2,1-7); 2 to Smyrna (2,8-11); 3 to Pergamum (2,12-17); 4 to Thyatira (2,18-28); 5 to Sardis (3,1-6); 6 to Philadelphia (3,7-13); 7 to Laodicea (3,14-22).

1. All the letters are presented in the same way and have identical sentences at their conclusion. The elements common to all are as follows:

At the beginning:

    a) "And to the angel of the Church which is at .... write:";

    b) "Here is what .... [a varying formula designating Christ] says";

    c) "I know ...".

At the end:

    "He who has ears, let him listen to that which the Spirit says to the Churches ...".

One can note in passing that the word Church forms an inclusion, for it is found in the introduction and in the conclusion. Inasmuch as all have a common framework, the seven letters can be bracketed as follows:

1	2	3	4	5	6	7

2. In all the letters the ending is composed of two elements, one unvarying, which we have just noted ("He who has ears ..."), the other quite variable, which is nevertheless always a promise to the "conqueror".

The promise to the conqueror begins with one participle (in Greek, "he-who-is-conquering") in all the letters, except in letter 4. Here, and only here, one has a long double formula, literally, "And he who conquers and he who keeps until the end my works" (2,26). This special characteristic suggests that this letter is to be distinguished from the others: it marks the central letter.

In the first three letters the promise to the conqueror comes *after* the unvarying sentence "He who has ears ...". In the four last, it comes *before* this sentence. Since the central letter is different from the others, the following outline results:

after			*special*	*before*		
1	2	3	4	5	6	7

In all the letters the promise to the conqueror begins with the nominative: "The conqueror ...", except in two letters where one finds a dative: "To the conqueror ...", letters 1 and 3. This detail leads one to think that these two letters are more closely related to each other.

3. One notes in most of the letters a call to conversion: "repent". But this call is lacking in letters 2 and 6. It has a special form in the central letter 4, where one finds explicitly the refusal to "repent". The absence of the verb in letters in 2 and 6 leads us to note that these two letters, and these alone, do not contain any reproof, nor any threat of punishment. We obtain the following arrangement:

no reproof:		2		6	
reproofs and "repent"	1	3	5	7	
Jezebel refuses to repent:		4			

Letters 2 and 6 are the only ones which speak of a "crown", the only ones also to contain an allusion to "the synagogue of Satan", "those who claim to be Jews but who are not" (2,9; 3,9). Their relationship is quite close then.

4. Between letters 1 and 3 we have already called attention to several resemblances. A more extended comparison shows that their outline is almost identical; the "I know ..." is followed by praise; then comes a "But I have against you ..." followed by reproaches, a "repent", a menacing "otherwise, I am coming to you". These two letters are the only ones which contain an allusion to the "Nicolaitans", who are mentioned only here (2,6.15) in the entire New Testament.

5. Letters 5 and 7 have the distinguishing characteristics of being the only ones to begin with blame. The "I know ..." is followed by no praise, only reproofs. The diagnosis which they make is similar: "You seem to be alive but you are dead" (3,1); "You think yourself rich ... you are wretched" (3,17). These contain terrible threats, above all 7 at 3,16. But after the call to conversion one finds also promises (3,4-5) and even promises which are most attractive (3,20-21). In addition, they are the only ones which do not mention any adversary of the Church.

6. We have already noted several characteristics peculiar to the central letter. It is possible to find still others. It is the longest letter of all and presents a special structure which gives it the appearance of a double letter. The other letters do not mention the word "Church" except at the beginning and at the end, in fixed formulae. Letter 4 has this word one additional time, and in a formula which is more solemn: "all the Churches", in the middle of its text (2,23). This sentence of 2,23 has the effect of a conclusion; it speaks of the Churches in the plural, as does the fixed sentence of the conclusion. But it contains also an element of the beginning, a designation of Christ similar to those which come regularly at the beginning of the letters after the formula "Here is what .... says"; this designation here is "the one who searches minds and hearts" (2,23). Then the name of the city is repeated (2,24) as at the beginning, introducing a second part of the letter.

The first part (2,18-23) has a structure similar in the beginning to that of letters 1 and 3: "I know ..." followed by praises and then "but I have against you" followed by reproofs. But then the structure takes a different turn (cf. above, paragraph 3) so as to open the possibility for a second part. This second part (2,24-28) resembles letters 2 and 6, for it contains neither reproofs nor threats. Thus the central letter witnesses to a synthesis of the various types of letters.

7. Our various observations can be summed up in the following concentric outline:

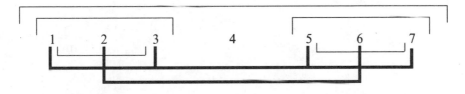

There is no denying that here is an arrangement harmonious in its very complexity.

What benefit do we gain from having made this discovery? First, we learn that the author of the Apocalypse was an accomplished artist who had a taste for polished arrangements. Then we realize that the Bible does not look askance at beauty. These points are not without interest.

Finally, we acquire a tool for analyzing. The outline really proves to be useful for better understanding the text as a whole and in its details. It shows that the seven letters do not constitute a random assembly, put together haphazardly, but a deliberately devised arrangement whose purpose is to provide a panorama of the varying situations which are found in the Christian communities.

The order of the letters witnesses to a refined pastoral sense. Letter 1 is perfectly suited for the beginning, for it begins with praise but follows with criticism and calls for an effort. Had letters 5 or 7 been placed at the beginning they would have proved offensive, for they begin with reproofs; letters 2 and 6 would not have succeeded in attracting attention, for they contain no criticism; one would have felt reassured at once! Still, where they are letters 2 and 6 are quite useful, for they show that perfection is possible. If John had written only of imperfect communities the picture would have been less challenging, for one would have been led to believe that complete fidelity is an unattainable ideal.

The same pastoral sense dictates the choice of the final letter. If placed at the end, letters 2 and 6 would have left too reassuring an impression: there is nothing to correct! John has placed at the end the letter which contains the harshest description of all (3,15-17) and the strongest threat (3,16). But he has taken care not to end the picture in an entirely negative way. On the contrary, in closing he discloses perspectives of intimacy with the Lord which are most attractive (3,20).

Chapter IV

A Deepening of Faith and of Christian Life

To judge by the analysis which we have just made, the Priestly Sermon (Heb 1,1 – 13,21) has been composed to be read aloud before a Christian assembly, doubtless like the one which St. Luke describes in Acts 20,7-8 or St. Paul in 1 Cor 14,26. The Christians have come together to hear the Word of God, to sing, to pray, and also, quite likely, to celebrate the Eucharist (cf. Acts 20,7; 1 Cor 11,20). Let us slip into their midst and hear the preaching addressed to them. It is as valid for us as it is for them.

N.B.: Before studying each section of this chapter the reader is advised to work through the passage of Hebrews given after the title.

1. Word of God and Action of God (Hebrews 1,1-4)

a) The Sermon is clearly connected with the liturgy of the Word of God. The preacher is well aware of this: we grasp it immediately, for his first words evoke the theme "God has spoken to us" (1,2). All throughout human history God has been concerned to enter into personal relationship with us: "On many occasions and in many ways he has spoken in times past to our fathers, and now, in this final stage where we are, he has spoken to us ...". There is something about this divine initiative, about God's perseverance, which fills us with wonder and confusion, but also with awesome gratitude: O Lord our God, who is man that you are interested in him?" (Ps 8,2.5; Heb 2,6). At the same time our sense of responsibility is awakened: the God who speaks to us has a right to our total attention! His word, we well know, is a seed which must be received in a heart well disposed (Luke 8,15) so as to yield fruit in abundance.

b) The liturgy of the Word is not all there is to the matter, for God is not content simply to speak: he has acted. He has intervened in an active way in our history. The Word of God is closely linked to this action which gives the Word all its validity. The Christian liturgy has two parts, inseparable the one from the other, one which proclaims the word, the other which makes present God's action. This action of God is his victory over sin and death, a victory gained through the passion of his Son. The beginning of the Sermon faithfully reflects this reality, for in one matchless sentence it presents in quick succession the Word of God and the mystery of Christ and ties them close together. Reduced to its main parts the sentence affirms that "God has spoken to us in his Son ... who ... having brought about the purification from sin is seated at His right". From now on the word of God reaches us in its fullness, because it has found its perfect form thanks to the incarnation of the Son of God, who is "splendor of His glory and imprint of His being" (1,3). From now on the action of God transforms our existence, for it unfolds for us completely and definitively in the glorifying Passion of Christ. It follows that for us the word of God and the action of God are inseparately linked to the mediation of Christ. It is in Christ that God speaks to us, it is in Christ that God saves us.

In this introductory sentence so rich in content, we notice that the author has not said one word about priesthood. But he has nonetheless prepared his subject in a way which is skillful and profound. We shall have the opportunity to see how.

2. A Traditional Explanation about Christ (Hebrews 1,5 – 2,18)

a) The sentence of introduction (1,1-4) ends with a contemplation of the present glory of Christ. The First Part (1,5 – 2,18) takes this contemplation as a point of departure. For it is to the risen Christ that God speaks the word of Ps 2 quoted in Heb 1,5: "My Son are you; I today have engendered you". In reading this psalm, which proclaims the coronation of the King-Messiah, the first Christians had the joy to discover a prophecy which was realized in the pascal event: Jesus, whose filial glory had been veiled during his earthly life, has been "constituted Son of God with power by his resurrection from the dead" (Rom 1,4; cf. Acts 13,33).

b) We must immediately observe that the beginning of the First Part does not constitute a special case in Hebrews. On the contrary, it is typical of the procedure used by the author. He always begins with the present state of the glorified Christ as he is known by faith.

Just as in the case of the First Part (1,5 – 2,18), the Second Part (3,1 – 5,10) begins by directing our gaze toward the present glory of Christ, a glory which is the basis of his authority. It is a glory greater than that of Moses (3,2), for it is that of the Son (3,6) while Moses was merely a servant (3,5).

In just the same way the long exposition of the central Third Part (7,1 – 10,18) begins by evoking the glorious role of our high priest. The person of Melchizedek, who symbolized this role beforehand, represented "the Son of God" (7,3). And the oracle of Ps 110 is applied to the "Son" who has been made perfect through his suffering (7,28; cf. 2,10; 5,8-9) and "elevated higher than the heavens" (7,26).

We see here what is for the author of Hebrews the fundamental premise which defines the Christian status: Christians know that they have a living relation with the risen Christ who is seated from now on at the right hand of God.

c) The First Part, as we have seen, is a brief doctrinal synthesis on the mystery of Christ. The preacher stays within traditional categories so that his listeners can follow him without difficulty. He straightaway refers to the lived experience of the Christian community, which contemplates in faith Christ glorified and recognizes in him its savior (1,5-14). He then recalls the way of suffering which Jesus followed to arrive at this glory (2,5-18). Passion and glorification of Christ Jesus: these are the two basic affirmations of the Christian message (cf. 1 Cor 15,3-4). They are usually presented in their chronological order. Our author prefers the inverse order which corresponds to the realistic approach he is following: from the present situation to its historical elucidation. This is the order found in the words of Peter as presented by St. Luke (Acts 3,13; 5,30) or in the sentence of St. Paul when he sets forth the movement of union towards Christ (Phil 3,10).

In order to describe Christ's glory the author cites the Old Testament (Heb 1,5-14). Placed in the light of the pascal event, the inspired texts become clear: they speak of Christ, of his relation with the Father, of his heavenly enthronement, of his power over the world. The texts cited in this section are for the most part connected with royal messianism, conformable to the early Christian tradition. The glorified Christ is the son of David for whom the oracle of the prophet Nathan is realized (Heb 1,5b – 2 Sam 7,14; 1 Chron 17,13) just as the parallel oracle of Ps 2 (Heb 1,5a – Ps 2,7; cf. Acts 13,33). He is the victorious king of whom Ps 45 speaks (Heb 1,8-9 – Ps 45,7-8). He is the Lord of Ps 110 whom God has invited to sit at His right (Heb 1,13 – Ps 110,1; cf. Matt 22,44; 26,64; Acts 2,34; 1 Cor 15,25; etc.). In him the messianic hopes are realized with unimaginable fullness, for he is at the same time the creator of heaven and earth (Heb 1,10 – Ps 102,26); his sovereignty is then complete (Heb 1,11-12 – Ps 102,27-28). He has a right not only to the titles of "Son" (1,5), of "First-Born" (1,6), of "Lord" (1,10), but also and equally to the very name "God" (1,8.9).

The name of Christ admits of still other aspects which it is important not to forget, for they have in no way been abolished by his glorification. The author recalls them in the second paragraph of his exposition (2,5-16). Christ is "man", "son of the human race" (2,6). To become "the forerunner of our salvation" (2,10) he became our "brother" (2,11-12). And brother he remains in his glory, for this glory crowned his sufferings which he accepted "for everyone" (2,9); it seals then forever his solidarity with us.

To evoke the Passion which glorified Jesus, the author makes use again of traditional texts: Ps 8 (Heb 2,6-9) which St. Paul cites with Ps 110 (1 Cor 15,25-27; Eph 1,20-22); Ps 22 (Heb 2,12) which, more than any other, is the psalm of the Passion (cf. Matt 27,35.39.43.46).

The theme of the superiority of Christ over the angels, a theme which the author uses in order better to unify this whole First Part, was familiar to Christians (cf. Eph 1,20-21; Col 1,16; 2,10.15; 1 Pet 3,22).

d) The doctrinal exposition of the First Part is then entirely traditional. It is only in bringing this part to its conclusion that the author opens new perspectives, in the sentence at 2,17 where he gives to Christ the title of "high priest". This innovation can be a source of surprise. But one would be mistaken, however, in judging it to constitute a break in the presentation. One should note, on the contrary, that it is introduced without the least trace of a clash and that it is in complete harmony with what has preceded (2,5-16). It is the most natural thing in the world to pass from the traditional treatment of the mystery of Christ to the priestly presentation of it, but only if the focus is on the essential purpose of priesthood and not on its ritual organization.

Priesthood, as we saw above (pp. 8-11), is intended to be a means of mediation. Viewed this way, should we not recognize that the glorified Christ, Son of God (1,5-14) and brother of men (2,5-16), is in an ideal position to be mediator? Through his Passion he has obtained for his humanity filial glorification close to God and, at the same time, he has linked himself to us in the most complete and most definitive manner possible by taking on himself our death. One with God and one with us, he is the perfect mediator or, in other words, the "high priest who is merciful and worthy of faith" (2,17).

To arrive at this position, the most necessary thing was that Christ make himself similar to us, for the other condition of the mediation, that which concerned his relations with God, was assured by the fact that he was Son of God. Hence the presentation of the theme of priesthood at 2,17 is more immediately connected with the explanation of the Passion. "To become high priest" Christ had to "make himself in all things like his brothers"; "in all things" means here: even unto trials, sufferings, and death.

We are led to recognize then that the arrangement of the First Part is admirably conceived to prepare the way for the introduction of the new theme. We add that the insistence on the angels, which at first sight can seem rather odd, is intelligible in the light of this orientation. For it was their capability as mediators which attracted the attention of the believers of this period. Were not the angels the beings best situated to serve as intermediaries between men and God? Jewish tradition gave them this role. Certain texts even assign to the most elevated among them the dignity of a heavenly high priest. By implicitly opposing such claims our author shows without stating it that Christ is much better qualified than any angel to fill the role of high priest. Son of God, he enjoys with his Father a relation much more intimate than any angel (1,5-14). Brother of men, he is much more capable of understanding us and of helping us (2,5-16). The angels assuredly have their place in the realization of the design of God, but it is a subordinate place (1,14). The glorified Christ is of incomparably more worth than they. He is for us more than a simple intermediary, for it is at the deepest level of his being that he is become for us, through his Passion, the true mediator between God and man.

e) Finally, is not "high priest" the title which expresses most perfectly the mystery of Christ? Such, in any case, is the thought which the author of Hebrews suggests as he brings his First Part to a close. The name which definitively sums up and completes all the others is "high priest merciful and worthy of faith" (2,17). One is justified in preferring it even to that of King-Messiah. In fact, the images of royal messianism are reconciliable only with difficulty to the mystery of Jesus. They are too often linked with political power and military triumphs. One can of course present the Passion as a victorious combat, but such a presentation partakes of the paradoxical and does not express the most profound aspects of the event. The priestly presentation, on the other hand, does not have these inconvenient aspects, for it is situated at a religious level and speaks of the establishing of a mediation. It places in evidence the necessity for the high priest of a close, twofold relation, with men and with God. The Passion of Christ appears necessary in order to establish a complete solidarity with men; his heavenly glorification is seen to be necessary in order to assure a perfect relation with God.

Other names express only this or that aspect of the situation and the being of Christ. "Son of God" expresses only his relation with God; "brother of men", only his relation with us; "Lord" evokes only his glory; "Servant", only his voluntary abasement. "High priest", on the other hand, gives an idea of the twofold relation and evokes simultaneously both Passion and glory. This title then offers distinct advantages. It was nevertheless too new for our author to be able to be content with a rapid presentation. He had to explain it again correctly; for it was open to being misunderstood. He also had to show methodically how well founded it was. It is to this task that he devotes himself in the following sections.

3. A Demonstration in Two Stages

Our analysis of the literary structure of Hebrews has shown us that the teaching of the priesthood of Christ is presented there in two successive parts, which constitute the Second and Third Parts of the sermon. Now we have to examine closer at hand the contents of these parts in order better to understand the way the argumentation unfolds.

The author proceeds in two stages, which follow a perfectly coherent order. He begins by showing that Christ is high priest: this is the subject matter of the Second Part (3,1 – 5,10). He then shows what type of "priesthood" is Christ's: this is the subject matter of the Third Part (5,11 – 10,39). He thus considers first (Second Part) the fundamental traits of priesthood and verifies their existence in Christ. He then interests himself (Third Part) in the specific traits by which the priesthood of Christ is different from previous forms of priesthood.

The point of reference is obviously the Old Testament. The author did not have to take into consideration pagan cults, for the question the early Christians were asking was, as we have seen, to know if Christ had "accomplished" all that was announced in the Old Testament. Is the accomplishment of the Old Testament priesthood to be found in the mystery of Christ? This was the problem which had to be resolved. If the reply is affirmative, it is all the more so with regard to pagan priesthoods, which represent a more mixed form of religion.

In order that there be an "accomplishment" of the priesthood of old in Christ, a relation of similarity between Christ and the Jewish high priests is indispensable (cf. the Excursus "The Three Conditions Necessary for the Fulfillment of the Scriptures", p. 54). The Second Part demonstrates clearly that the relation exists. It is interesting to note the author's technique. He is careful not to examine external details. He does not consider any of the ceremonies prescribed for the consecration of the high priest: ritual bath, anointing, sacred vestments, offerings of animals (Exod 29; Lev 8). Nor does he dwell on any of the rites which the high priest was called upon to perform. He goes at once to the heart of the matter: he considers the two essential traits which condition the exercise of the priesthood. A high priest must be 1) "accredited for relations with God"; 2) "merciful" towards men. It is easy to see that there is no question here of virtues involving only an individual, such as courage or moderation. "Accreditation for relations with God" and "mercy" are virtues involving relations between persons, with God on one side and with men on the other. Their presence in a representative of the human family constitutes the necessary and sufficient condition for speaking about priesthood. A man filled with compassion for those like himself but who does not have access to God is not equipped to be priest: he cannot represent his brothers with God. From this point of view his compassion remains sterile. On the other hand, a person admitted into God's intimacy, but placed beyond solidarity with men, cannot be a priest: he does not represent men; his lofty position does nothing to change their condition. He alone is priest who at one and the same time is linked intimately to men by all the fibres of his human nature and fully accredited with God. Such a one will guarantee his brothers and sisters a good relationship with God and thus transform their existence. This explains why the author has presented together both aspects of priesthood — in 2,17 — and why he made it the subject of the two sections of the same part. Commentators who break up this part to impose on Hebrews a different division (cf. above, p. 19), not only disfigure the literary form of the work, they also prevent understanding the author's thought on a fundamental point.

4. An Authorized High Priest (Hebrews 3,1–4,14)

a) The first aspect developed is that which concerns the relation with God. Jesus has a right to the title of high priest for he is "authorized with Him who has installed him" (3,2). Most translations commit an error here, for they speak of "fidelity" and say that Jesus is "faithful to Him who installed him". The Greek word in question certainly has this meaning in other contexts, but its first meaning is "worthy of faith", and in this passage (3,1-6) it is certainly the first meaning which should be retained. For the author is referring to a text of the Old Testament (Num 12,7) where the word has this first meaning. What is affirmed in it is not the fidelity of Moses but his credibility, his authority as representative of God, an authority based on his intimate relation with God (Num 12,1-8). Christ glorified deserves the same qualification as Moses, and with even more reason, for "he has been judged worthy of a glory superior to that of Moses" (3,3). Moses had his place *in* God's house, as a servant (3,5); but Christ has authority *over* God's house, for he is the Son (3,6) and has the title of builder (3,3; cf. 2 Sam 7,13-14). The house of God which Christ constructs is composed of living stones (cf. 1 Pet 2,5; Eph 2,21-22), in which we, the believers, are integrated (Heb 3,6), on the condition that we remain faithful to our vocation.

b) The author as a matter of course adds here an exhortation describing the consequences which result for us from the position of Christ glorified (3,7 – 4,14).

Inasmuch as Christ has full priestly authority, and inasmuch as he speaks to us from his vantage point of proximity to God, we should receive his word with faith. He will lead us into "God's rest". A passage from Ps 95 provides the basic text: "Today, if you hear his voice, do not harden your heart ...". This text is all the more appropriate for it maintains the parallel between Christ and Moses, recalling certain events of the Exodus.

Here a bit of precision is in order. It is sometimes said that the author here compares the Christian life to the long journey of the Israelites in the desert. This could be accurate if the psalm had been cited in Hebrew, for then one would have found mention of Massa and of Meriba (Exod 17,1-7; Num 20,1-13). But it is the Greek translation which our author uses. Now in the Greek translation the proper names disappear and the only allusions which one can recognize all refer to one definite episode, which occurred *before* the long wandering of forty years in the desert. The biblical account of this event is placed right after the text of Num 12 from which the author has just drawn (Heb 3,5 – Num 12,7).

After setting out from Egypt under the guidance of Moses, the Israelites at first stayed in the Sinai, but God urged them on towards the Promised Land so that they would take possession of it (cf. Deut 1,6-8). Once they had drawn near their goal they sent out a group to reconnoiter (Num 13). The group returned with a report which was both enthusiastic and discouraging. The Promised Land is a wonderful place, but the inhabitants are formidable (Num 13,27-28). What should the Israelites do? Two attitudes are possible: 1) An attitude of faith in God's word; this is what Moses suggests: "Look, the Lord your God has given you this country. Go up and take possession of it as the Lord, the God of your ancestors, has said: do not be afraid and do not waver" (Deut 1,20; cf. Num 14,7-9). 2) An attitude of defiance, which deviates from God's word and lets itself be mesmerized by the difficulties of the enterprise: "They are a people taller and stronger than we, their cities are immense and their walls reach up to the sky" (Deut 1,28; cf. Num 13,32-33). Had they gone on ahead with faith the Israelites would have entered into the Promised Land; but they did not trust God; for this they were condemmed to wander in the desert and to die there (Num 14,32-33).

Christians now face the same alternatives. The Kingdom of God is before them, near enough to touch, with its peace, its joy, its blessings. Christ, who opened up the way, invites them to take possession of it immediately, in faith. They hear his voice which the Gospel proclaims; "The Kingdom of God is at hand, change your heart and believe in the good news" (Mark 1,14; cf. Heb 4,2). Two attitudes are possible: to have faith and enter ("for we enter into the Rest, we believers", Heb 4,3), or to refuse to believe and be excluded. The fate of the Israelites condemmed to wander constitutes an impressive warning. The conclusion is obvious: "Let us press on then to enter into the Rest ..." (4,11). "Since we have an eminent high priest who has penetrated the heavens, Jesus, the Son of God, let us hold fast to the profession of faith" (4,14).

This entire exhortation shows clearly how the author links closely the themes of Word of God and priesthood of Christ. Far from omitting the ministry of the Word from among the prerogatives of Christ the high priest, he insists on it here by putting it in first place. And he presents this ministry as taking place: it is *now* that Christ, the high priest fully approved by God in glory, hands on to us the divine word capable of saving us, a word which we must accept in faith.

c) As regards the relation between the priesthood of Christ and the word, a question arises: why has the author chosen to compare here Christ with Moses, and not with the high priest Aaron? The answer is simple: in the matter at hand Moses seems to be more representative in the Bible than his brother. There is nothing surprising in the fact that a Jewish author such as Philo attributed to Moses the fullness of the priesthood. In fact, the Old Testament knew no mediator of the word superior to Moses; this is exactly what the text of Num 12,1-8 (cited in Heb 3,2-5) states. On this point the Jewish priests were dependent upon Moses: for he is the one who, according to Deut 31,9, had entrusted to them the divine instructions, with the command to transmit them to the people. To show in Christ the definitive accomplishment of this aspect of priesthood, it was logical and necessary to take as point of reference the position of Moses and not that of the priestood of old which was inferior to Moses. The author has no difficulty in showing that to speak to us in the name of God and to introduce us into God's intimacy, if we let him, the glorified Christ has an authority not only equal to by superior to that of Moses.

Excursus: The Three Conditions Necessary for the Fulfillment of the Scriptures

a) To recognize in the New Testament the fulfillment of the Old, three conditions must be met. The first, most basic, is the existence of a relationship of resemblance and of continuity between them. If the new reality which claims to follow upon the old is without any relationship to it, we cannot speak of fulfillment. It would be more correct to speak rather of innovation pure and simple, and it would be impossible to situate this innovation in the plan of God prepared and foretold long before. Let us suppose, for example, that a gospel had presented to us as savior a man of pagan origin and with absolutely no relationship with the lineage of Abraham, the tribe of Judah, and the family of David. Clearly the messianic promises stated in the Bible would not be recognized and fulfilled in him.

b) The second condition — and this would not occur to one spontaneously — is that the new reality *not* be like the old in all ways. Otherwise one would always remain on the level of preparation instead of passing to that of definitive realization. For example, if Jesus had been a successor of David just like Solomon or Josiah, that is, exercising power on earth for the length of his mortal life, one would not be able to recognize in him the perfect fulfillment of the messianic promises. A divine fulfillment is never a simple repetition of that which has already taken place. It always brings with it differences and breaks, for it is situated on a different level.

c) This different level is, of course, a higher level. This is the third condition required for fulfillment. The differences perceived have to do away with the limitations and the imperfections of the past; they must tend clearly forward in an advance which is at once decisive and unforeseeable, showing forth the creative intervention of God. Otherwise one would be faced with a variation of questionable value. Thus the rebuilding of the Temple after the Exile, although different in many ways from the building which Solomon constructed, did not constitute the definitive fulfillment of God's intention to dwell in the midst of his people, for the differences were of minor importance and did not tend in the direction of progress (cf. Hag 2,1-3). A new intervention of God was therefore to be expected (Hag 2,6-9).

Resemblance, difference, superiority or, in other words, continuity, break, pre-eminence: these are the three types of relationship always present in true fulfillment between the new reality which the fulfillment establishes and the former preparation which it brings to an end. There are countless examples in the New Testament.

Suggested assignment: in Hebrews it is useful to trace the three types of relationship in 8,1 – 9,28. Or between the Passion and Resurrection of Jesus on the one hand and on the other the history of Abel (Gen 4; cf. Heb 11,4; 12,24); or the sacrifice of Abraham (Gen 22; cf. Heb 11,17-19); or the story of Joseph (Gen 37; 42-45); or between the Christian Church (1 Pet 2,5-10) and the Temple of Solomon (1 Kgs 5,16 – 6,38), etc.

---

5. A High Priest Who Is One with Humans (Hebrews 4,15 – 5,10)

The extraordinary authority of Christ, his position at the right of God, could create the impression that he is now in a position too lofty to concern himself with the lot of humans. This authority and position could inspire a paralyzing fear: how could one dare enter into relation with a being so glorious and so holy? In fact union with God in glory is not a sufficient foundation for the priesthood. The other aspect has to be linked to it: the capacity to relate with humanity. This capability is assuredly not lacking in the glorified Christ. The author says as much at the beginning of the second section (4,15) and invites us also to come forward immediately with "full assurance" (4,16). Now that Christ is seated there, the throne of God is no more a source of danger for those who draw near (cf. Isa 6,1-5; Exod 19,21); it has become "the throne of grace" (Heb 4,16), for Christ is our brother who knows by experience our state of weakness and is there to help us.

a) In order to develop the second theme the author gives a definition of "every high priest" (5,1-4) and immediately proceeds to apply it to Christ (5,5-10). There is no question of a full definition; the definition given leaves aside the aspect of authority already mentioned in 3,1-6 in order to insist exclusively on the aspect of solidarity. The high priest is "taken from among humans" and he is "appointed in favor of humans for relations with God" (5,1). It is in this perspective that the author speaks of the offering of sacrifices: he perceives in the regulations of the ancient ritual the sign of a profound solidarity between the high priest and the people. The high priest belongs to the same race, with all its weaknesses and sins. The Bible is witness to all this, for it prescribes that the high priest "offer for himself as well as for the people sacrifices for sin" (5,3; cf. Lev 9,7-8; 16,6.11). It is in this perspective again that the author recalls the need of a call from God (5,4): one does not make a high priest of oneself in arrogantly raising oneself above others (cf. Num 16–17); on the contrary, admittance to the priesthood requires an attitude of humility before God, an attitude through which one remains united to others.

In applying this to Christ (5,5-10) it is this last point which at once is taken up in accordance with the technique of concentric development. Christ has shown himself to be one with men for he has taken an attitude of humility: "he did not glorify himself" as the author says literally (many translations are a bit wide of the Greek text). It is God his Father who named him high priest as Scripture testifies (Heb 5,6 – Ps 110,4). Later on the text (Heb 5,7-8) describes in a fashion more precise the road of humility and of human solidarity which has brought Christ to the priesthood. It is a moving recollection of the Passion of Christ, a recollection which recalls in particular his prayer at Gethsemani (Matt 26,37-44 and parallels) as well as his loud cries on the cross (Matt 27,46.50; Mark 15,33.37). There one sees that Christ truly shared to the very end our human condition with all that that implies as regards suffering and affliction. In the grip of agony because of imminent death he prays, he begs, he cries out, he weeps (5,7). He is truly "surrounded on all sides by weakness" (cf. 5,2) and his situation corresponds then to what "every high priest" (5,1) must accept in order to be capable of true compassion.

b) But the role of high priest does not consist simply in sharing in human misery; it consists above all in transforming the situation by means of an offering of sacrifice. This aspect of offering is not lacking in the case of Christ no more than the transformation which takes place. Christ "has made an offering" and "he has been heard".

What then did he offer? He offered "prayers and supplications with a loud cry and tears to Him who could save him from death"

(5,7). The dramatic events which place the life of Jesus in jeopardy and with it his life's work and even the revelation of his person (cf. Matt 27,40), these events have become the stuff of offering because they have been faced in intense prayer. The object of this prayer is not specified, but we can infer that it has to do with changing the course of events and triumphing over death. Jesus' prayer was vehement and accompanied by cries. But it did not take the form of an ultimatum imposed on God. It remained authentic prayer, penetrated through and through with "religious respect" (this is the last word of v. 7; it corresponds to what the Bible calls "fear of God"). This prayer left the door open to divine initiative, and this is why it could be heard and why in fact it was heard. The offering of Christ was accepted, the course of events was transformed.

But the hearing of Christ's prayer took a paradoxical form: it is in dying that Christ triumphed over death (cf. 2,14)! The event was not changed from without, through a miraculous divine intervention, but from within, thanks to the adherence of Christ to the transforming action of God. The prayer of Christ in agony was a dialogue with the Father which ended in a union of wills (cf. Matt 26,42) and in a realization of a common work (cf. John 16,32). The Father hears the Son while the Son fulfills the will of the Father. The author of Hebrews sets forth this mystery by describing the Passion in two different ways which at first sight may seem to be incompatible but which in reality are complementary: he describes it as both a prayer which has been heard and as a painful act of obedience. Christ "offered prayers ... and was heard" (5,7), but at the same time "he has learned by his sufferings obedience" (5,8). We find here a profound revelation of the mystery of Christ, a source of inexhaustible light for the Christian's life of prayer.

c) The final sentence of this text (5,9-10) expresses the result of the obedient offering of Christ: this offering makes him the perfect high priest. There has taken place not only a transformation of the event which, instead of ending in catastrophe, has ended in triumph, but — and this is more important — in the event the very humanity of Jesus has been transformed. In accepting the paroxysm of human suffering and in opening it up to God's action Christ has been "made perfect" (we shall have to return to this expression later on) and has become "cause of eternal salvation" for all those who accept his guidance. In other words, he has become the perfect mediator. And this is easy to understand if one pauses a moment to reflect on what happened: in his Passion Christ went beyond all limits in obeying his Father and in exercising solidarity with his brothers and sisters. In so acting he has brought to unsurpassed perfection his relation with God and his relation with men and sealed these two relations together at the deepest level of his being. A divine proclamation verifies the fact: at the end of the Passion Christ is "proclaimed by God high priest after the manner of Melchizedek" (5,10). The prophetic oracle of Ps 110 has found its accomplishment. By the path of humble solidarity Christ has come to priesthood.

d) Thus the author brings to an end the first stage of his demonstration. And a convincing stage it is. Let us note again that in order to make his argumentation effective he has taken into account only elements which are essential. In his description of the priesthood of old (5,1-4) he has inserted no specific detail about the rite of consecration of the high priest. He was content to use the vaguest expression possible: "Every high priest ... is appointed ..." (5,1). In like manner he refrains from specifications about sacrifices, avoiding mention of the fact that the Jewish priests offered animal victims.

In addition, here as already in 2,17-18, he has insisted on a condition which is nowhere emphasized in the Old Testament: that of the bonds which the high priest should have with other men. The Old Testament, as shown above (pp. 10-11), was concerned rather with indicating the things which separated him from other men in order to secure in this way a better relation between the high priest and God (cf. Deut 32,9). The resemblance of the high priest with men was all too clear and if anything was too close: the high priest was a sinner as was everyone else. This was seen from the time of Aaron himself (cf. Exod 32,1-4). It was appropriate to gloss over this unfortunate state of affairs. Instead of speaking of solidarity and of mercy as conditions for the priesthood, severity was required against sinners and the refusal to compromise with them (Exod 32,25-29; Num 25,6-13). The idea of approaching the priesthood by way of humility never occurred to the Jews. On the contrary, it was with pleasure that the unusual dignity of God's chosen one was exalted (Sir 45,6-13; 50,5-11), and the role of the high priest was naturally thought to be the summit of a series of promotions. To reach it some ambitious persons did not hesitate to use any means available (cf. 2 Macc 4). Still and all, an attentive reading of the biblical text shows that solidarity with men is required for the exercise of the priesthood and that God himself had blocked the approach to the arrogant (Num 16–17). In the light of Christ's Passion the author of Hebrews re-read the ancient texts and discovered these aspects.

e) With the same stroke he completed his demonstration. In order to recognize Christ as high priest he had started, as we saw, from the current status of Christ and of Christians. Christ is now with God and he puts us in contact with God by integrating us into his own body. He is therefore our mediator and he, more than anyone else, has a right to the title of high priest.

To be really valid this first demonstration had to be completed by a reflection on Christ's becoming priest and confirmed by an explicit word of God. It does not suffice to affirm that Christ is now our mediator; it is appropriate to show how he established this mediation, for the most important element of priesthood is precisely this: the action by which the high priest establishes communication between the people and God (cf. above, p. 11). If it could be thought that there was nothing of the sort in all that Christ had experienced there would be reason to place in doubt his qualifying as high priest. Furthermore, in this area personal reflexion is not enough. Otherwise the proposed doctrine would be only one more human interpretation of the history of salvation and would be open to discussion. On the other hand, if the proposal can lay claim to the explicit witness of Scripture, then it will be clear that there is question of divine revelation.

The section which we have just read (4,15 – 5,10) provides all these elements. It shows not only that Christ has placed himself in complete solidarity with human distress, but also that by his manner of confronting events he has transformed them into an offering ("he has offered") which has established a mediation ("he has become a cause of salvation"). In addition, the author has found an argument from Scripture whose value is indisputable. It was sufficient for him to take Ps 110, recognized by the Church as a messianic psalm which proclaims the glorification of Christ (cf. Matt 22,44; 26,64; etc.) and to pass from verse 1 (cited in Heb 1,12) to verse 4 in order to show that the Christ who is enthroned at the right hand of God (Ps 110,1) has also been proclaimed priest by God (Ps 110,4; Heb 5,6).

The lived experience of Christians who see themselves united to God thanks to the glorified Christ, reflections on the events of the Passion which lead to the recognition that a mediation has been established, a solemn witness of the Word of God in Ps 110: these are, in Hebrews, the three bases of the demonstration of the priesthood of Christ. One can hardly object that the demonstration lacks a solid foundation!

6. A Priesthood Which is Different (Hebrews 7,1-28)

Well aware of the three dimensions of the fulfillment of the Scriptures, the author of Hebrews continues his presentation with a

Third Part (5,11 – 10,39) in which he shows that the priesthood of
Christ is quite different from the priesthood of old and that this
latter is now outdated. This is a new point of view which was not
explicitly mentioned in the Second Part (3,1 – 5,10).

a) When the author cited in the preceding section (4,14 – 5,10)
the divine proclamation of Ps 110,4, he used it in a general sense to
show that Christ has been named priest by God exactly as was
Aaron (5,4-6). Now, in 7,1-28, he takes up the same text to subject
it to a detailed examination and makes use of it to prove that Christ
is a priest in a fashion quite different from that of Aaron. The psalm
says in fact "priest after the manner of Melchizedek". What does
this description entail? The author establishes the meaning by going
back to the text concerning Melchizedek at Gen 14,18-20. To be
precise, he does not produce a verse-by-verse comment. His
procedure consists rather in establishing a relationship, without
saying as much explicitly, among the ancient episode described in
Genesis, the oracle of the psalm, and the present role of the glorified
Christ.

In this way he finds that the text of Gen 14 gives a description
of Melchizedek which resembles in advance Christ glorified. For the
text presents Melchizedek as a priest with no mention of "father or
mother or genealogy". The fact is odd, for in the Old Testament
family ancestry was of decisive importance for the priesthood (cf.
Ezra 2,62). The text of Gen 14 does not speak of the birth of
Melchizedek nor of his death and thus does not set him within the
limits of any given time. The author takes advantage of this failure
to mention limits and suggests the figure of a priest who takes part
in the divine eternity and will always be a priest. In brief, a priest
who would be at the same time the Son of God (7,1-3). Lack of
priestly genealogy and perpetual priesthood: such are the two traits
which define the priesthood "after the manner of Melchizedek".
The author will keep coming back to this view all through the
section (cf. for the first trait 7,5-6.13.14.16a, and for the second
7,8.16b-17.23-25.28).

Other elements in the text of Gen 14 allow the author to show
that Melchizedek is in a situation of superiority with regard to
Abraham and thus also with regard to the Jewish priests who are
the descendants of Abraham (7,4-10).

By this analysis of Gen 14 the author of Hebrews has
undermined the traditional belief of the Jews who attributed to the
levitical priesthood the highest possible value. He has shown in fact
that before even speaking of the birth of Levi, the Bible had already
sketched the figure of a priest both different and superior.

b) The author then passes to the oracle of Ps 110,4 and this time takes the offensive against the ancient institutions, the Jewish priesthood, and the Mosaic Law. This paragraph of Hebrews (7,11-28) contains more than one difficulty; nevertheless, the basic argument is quite simple: the author observes that in proclaiming prophetically the perpetual priesthood of a different priest — one who would obviously take the place of the levitical priests — the psalm's oracle shows the provisional and imperfect character of the ancient priesthood. By the same title the entire edifice of the institutions of old is destined for ruin, for the priesthood was the keystone of everything (7,12). "On the one hand there is the abrogation of the previous precept by reason of its insufficiency... and, on the other hand, the introduction of a better hope", a hope which introduces a priesthood which is fully sufficient (7,18-19).

To develop his case the author considers the question of the value of the priestly consecration in the Old Testament. And it is at this point that a problem of vocabulary complicates matters for the modern reader. In the Greek translation of the Old Testament the rites prescribed for the conferral of the priesthood are not called "consecration" of priests nor "ordination" but "perfection" (*teleiōsis*), that is to say, "action which makes perfect", "action which gives perfection" *. Our author clearly is of the opinion that this word is well chosen, for a true priestly consecration must transform profoundly the one who receives it to such a degree that nothing in him can now displease God. His role of mediator requires this. Priestly consecration must therefore confer perfection. The priest's position with God depends on this, and also his power to intervene in favor of the people.

Now in announcing implicitly the removal of the ancient priesthood, the oracle of the psalm infers that in the Old Testament the priestly consecration did not deserve the name. It was not really an "action which confers perfection": it did not guarantee the priest a good relation with God. Otherwise God would have had no reason to raise up a new type of priest (7,11). In fact, God has "raised up" (the same Greek word means also "bring back to life")

---

* Greek words involving the root *telei-* can be translated into English with words involving either the English word "perfect" (e.g., "to perfect", "to bring to perfection", "perfect", "perfecter") or the English word "fulfill" (e.g., "to fulfill", "to bring to fulfillment", "fulfilled", "fulfiller"). In the first part of the present study words related to "perfect" tend to be used; in the structured translation, words related to "fulfill". No difference in meaning is intended by this difference in usage.

a completely different priest, one who is not of the priestly tribe of Levi but of the non-priestly tribe of Judah (7,13-14) and who has not received the priesthood by hereditary succession but thanks to the glorifying transformation of his resurrection (7,16).

c) The priesthood of Christ, guaranteed by God's oath in the psalm, is undeniably superior to that of the Jewish priests (7,20-22); his is an unending priesthood — "the risen Christ will no more die" (Rom 6,9) — whereas theirs was limited by death (Heb 7,23-25). The position of Christ as priest, proclaimed by the psalm, clearly towers above that of the Jewish high priests. The latter remained mortal men, imperfect and sinful (7,28). The ceremonies meant to "perfect" them brought no change; these ceremonies were not efficacious (7,18) and did not free them from the need of starting again the endless round of their offerings (7,27). The psalm's oracle, on the contrary, sets before our eyes the figure of a priest truly accepted by God "for all times". In him is realized what the Bible sketched out in speaking of Melchizedek: a priest who is Son of God and who thus enjoys the most intimate relation imaginable with God. His consecration has not remained inefficacious. It has truly been an "action which makes perfect". Such is the conclusion of this section (7,28). It can be paraphrased in the following terms: "While the Law of Moses constituted as high priests men who remained lacking, the oracle of Ps 110 constituted as high priest a man who at the same time is Son of God. This man has been consecrated high priest forever by means of an action which has truly transformed him and which has made him perfect".* What this transforming action consisted in is stated briefly by the author at the end of v. 27, but these few words cannot suffice. They do no more than prepare the following section (8,1 – 9,28).

---

* The sentence of Heb 7,28 provides us with an occasion for making a remark valid for the other sections of the Third Part as well. It is to be noted that in order to criticize the Old Testament priesthood the author of Hebrews relies upon the Old Testament itself. It is thus clear that if he denies the value of the Old Testament in one sense, he recognizes it in another. He acknowledges its prophetic value and denies its institutional value. He shows that the Old Testament as prophecy announces the abrogation of the Old Testament as Law. Or, in other words, the Old Testament as revelation predicts the end of the Old Testament as institution. This is precisely the position of Saint Paul such as is found, for example, in Rom 3,1: "Now, without passing through the Law [here we see the end of the Old Testament as institution], the justice of God has been made manifest in conformity to the witness of the Law and of the prophets [value of the Old Testament as revelation]". This position follows exactly from the logic of "fulfillment" (cf. pp. 54-55).

7. The Sacrifice Which Makes Perfect (Hebrews 8–9)

Taking up the final statement of Chapter 7, the central section (8,1 – 9,28) invites us to consider the way which Christ followed in order to arrive at his present position of high priest acceptable to God. This way is that of sacrificial offering of a completely new type by means of which Christ has truly been "made perfect". Personal transformation, offering carried out, way followed: these are three different expressions to convey what has been realized in the unique event of the Passion of Christ.

a) The author had already spoken of this even in the Second Part (cf. 5,1-10), but in a perspective of continuity with the priesthood of old and hence without dwelling on the differences. He now takes up the subject again and with no further ado tells his listeners that he has arrived at the "main point of the explanation" (8,1). We shall not be surprised at this evaluation, for we noted earlier that in the outline of priestly mediation the crucial moment is that of the rising phase (cf. p. 11). Everything depends on the efficacy of this crucial moment.

In order to call to mind the sacrificial activity of "every high priest" the author was satisfied in 5,1-4 to use general expressions. They have enabled him to note the resemblances with the mystery of Christ, for Christ also "has offered" (5,7). Now he considers details and points out contrasts. The "liturgy" which is proper to Christ is "quite different" from the ancient sacrificial cult (8,6). The author successively examines: a) the level at which the old cult took place (8,4-5); b) the covenant which was associated with it (8,7.13); c) the precise organization of this cult (9,1-10). To the old institutions he opposes in inverse order: c′) the development of Christ's sacrifice (9,11-14); b′) the foundation of the new covenant (9,15-17); a′) the level attained by Christ (9,24-28).

We should note that the two subdivisions which pertain to the theme of the covenant (b and b′) call to mind both old and new covenant, the first subdivision (8,7-13) in a perspective of opposition, the second subdivision (9,14-23) in a perspective of similarity.

b) The most meaningful subdivisions are those of the center (c: 9,10; c′: 9,11-14) for they treat the main subject matter: the sacrificial activity itself. The author recalls the old system of ritual separations which we have described above (pp. 10-11). A sacred place has been established. It consists of a holy part, the "first tent" (9,2), and a "most holy" part (9,3), thought to be the dwelling place of God or "sanctuary". The people are not allowed to enter in either for they do not have the "holiness" needed. The priests may enter into the "first tent" (9,6) which is like the way of access to the "sanctuary", but they may not enter into the latter. Only the high priest is authorized to do that, by reason of his special consecration, but even he functions under severe restrictions: he must limit his entrance to once a year, and the condition for entering is a sacrificial offering (9,7). The ceremony to which the author alludes is that of the Day of Expiation (Yom Kippur, Lev 16), the high point of the Jewish liturgy.

The question which suggests itself is the mediation value of this solemn liturgy. From this depends the judgment to be given about the system as a whole. If an authentic relation is established with God, then the system is excellent. But if the contrary is true, then it can only constitute a provisional solution, one to be set aside as soon as a better one is found.

The diagnosis of the author is pitiless: the old liturgy was powerless to establish mediation. The very prescriptions of the ritual attest the fact, for after the sacrifice just as before, all separations must be maintained. It should be noted that these prescriptions, formulated in the Bible, are part of the inspired text. Therefore it is the Holy Spirit in person who reveals, by means of the texts, that the ancient liturgy did not attain its goal (9,8). It came to a dead end. In fact, it was not into the dwelling of God that the Jewish high priest entered but into a material, human building (cf. 9,1.24), and God does not dwell in human constructions (cf. Acts 7,48; 17,24). The "first tent", unfortunately, was unable to provide access to anything else, for it was itself of human devising. A conclusion follows: "the way of the sanctuary was still not manifest as long as the first tent existed" (9,8).

c) The underlying reason for this no-win situation is attributed by the author to be the nature of the sacrifices offered (9,9). Even if the true way had been known, drawing near to God was impossible because there was no sacrifice worthy to be presented to God: we draw near to God not by walking but by offering.

The criticism which the author makes as regards the sacrifices of old is revealing. It offers an unexpected perspective on the purpose of sacrificial offering. Instinctively we think of this offering as a means of pleasing God and of winning his favors. We try somehow to have God change his attitude towards us. The author invites us to take the opposite point of view; he shows that the effect of the sacrifice should be to transform the one who offers, rather than the one to whom the offering is made. The ancient ritual offerings were lacking in value because they were "incapable of

THE SACRIFICE WHICH MAKES PERFECT

rendering perfect in conscience the one who performed the act of cult" (9,9). They were merely "external rites" (literally, "rites of flesh") connected with an entire system of observances concerning foods, drinks, and washings (9,10).

What is needed for a person to be able to enter into relation with God is a profound transformation of his being which makes him perfect in his conscience. At this level the old rites were entirely ineffective.

The author will complete his thought later on (10,4-6): the old sacrifices, made up of the offerings of immolated animals, were unable to achieve mediation. What relation, really, could there be between the blood of a slain animal and the conscience of a person? "It is impossible that the blood of bulls and goats take away sins" (10,4). Further, what communion was possible between a dead animal and the living God? More than once the Old Testament had expressed God's disgust for this type of cult (cf. Heb 10,5-7 – Ps 40,7-9). Contact was not established from either side. When all was said and done the old system remained fixed in separation: separation of people from priest, separation of priest from the victim offered, separation of victim from God. The separations were unavoidable, for the priest was unable to offer himself to God: sinner that he was, he was both unworthy and incapable.

The result was that mediation was not achieved. The ancient cult remained necessarily confined at a level at once earthly and figurative, as the author notes in the first subordinate division (8,5). The covenant associated with this cult was necessarily defective, as he notes in the second subordinate division (8,7-9). Not being based on an act of mediation which was really valid, the old covenant suffered from the same weakness as the cult itself, that of being completely external. The religious plight of the people of the Old Testament corresponded then to the following outline:

people | priest | victim | God

d) Then comes Christ (9,11). His sacrifice changes the situation completely and at the same time puts an end to the entire ancient system of ritual separations. The author does not repeat here the description of the event which he made at 5,7-8, but he sets forth its meaning and shows how the offering of Christ was different from the sacrifices of old and how it surpassed them.

He affirms in a triumphal tone that Christ has brought about that which no high priest was able to do: "he entered once for all into the sanctuary" (9,12). Postponing until later the precisions pertaining to the sanctuary (9,24), he defines at once the two means that allowed Christ to enter it (9,11-12). These means are exactly parallel to those which were just mentioned for the old cult: 1) a way of access; 2) a sacrificial offering.

The way of access is a "tent" (9,11), which has replaced "the first tent" criticized in 9,8. The sacrificial offering consists in "the very blood" of Christ (9,12) which replaces "the blood of goats and of calves", that is to say, the sacrifices criticized in 9,9.

The second means is clearly indicated and its value will be explained in greater detail in the following sentence (9,14). In contrast, the first means seems less easy to identify. Some commentators think that in speaking of "the tent" the author has in view the heavens which Christ has traversed (cf. 4,14). Such an interpretation is so poor in doctrinal content that it does not help us to understand the exceptional importance which the author attributes to this term for approaching God: he mentions it at the very center of the text (cf. above, p. 36), and he describes it in a most emphatic way. On the other hand, this interpretation does not agree with what had just been said in 9,8: the way of access to the sanctuary was not "manifest" at the time of the first tent. Now the idea that it was necessary to pass through the heavens to arrive at God was something known at the time. There was no need to wait for Christ in order to discover it.

Since there is question here of the way in which the Temple has been replaced in the mystery of Christ it is appropriate to seek for illumination in what the Gospel tradition has to say on the subject. We should remind ourselves that this tradition existed before our Gospels reached the stage of final editing and our author could not ignore it in a matter of such primary importance. In the Gospel tradition the theme of the new Temple occupies a prominent place. It is directly linked with the death and resurrection of Jesus (Matt 26,61; Mark 14,58; John 2,13-22). The way in which our author speaks of "the greater and more perfect tent" corresponds closely to what the Gospels suggest: Jesus, by his death and resurrection, has established a new Temple, not material but spiritual, which makes it possible for believers really to enter into a relation with God. St. John explicitly states what the others give to understand: this new Temple is nothing else than the body of the risen Christ (John 2,21).

We are thus brought to a profound interpretation of our text (Heb 9,11): to enter into the glory of the Father, Jesus himself, as man, had need of a transformation of his humanity. This transformation was achieved in his Passion. It is through his transformed humanity that Christ is from now on in relation with God. This humanity then takes the place of "the first tent" whose function was to provide access to the sanctuary. Let us add at once: "the greater and more perfect tent" is obviously not a means of access reserved for the exclusive use of Christ. Quite the contrary, it was set up for us. All of us are invited to enter into it in order to find union with God (cf. 10,19-22). But Christ is the one who set up the tent (cf. 3,3) and who inaugurated this way (10,20).

e) The existence of this new means of approach is inseparable from the sacrificial offering of Christ. The author shows this by closely uniting the mention of the tent to that of the blood, in the same grammatical construction. He states that "Christ ... by the tent ... and ... by his blood has entered into the sanctuary" (9,11-12). It is in fact by his offering to God that the humanity of Jesus has been transformed. What the sacrifices of old were intrinsically incapable of bringing about (cf. 9,9) this offering achieved. It made Christ "perfect" (cf. 7,28; 5,9; 2,10) in such a way that his humanity is from now on "the more perfect tent" which sets up a relation with God. In 5,7 the author has described the offering of Christ by saying that Christ "has offered prayers and supplications ...". Going one step further, he states in 9,14 that Christ "offered himself to God". This is a new way, a very precise new way, of expressing the profound reality of the event portrayed at 5,7-8: in his prayer of supplication Christ opened his whole being as man to the transforming action of God and he accepted to learn obedience through his sufferings. In this way he "offered himself to God" and was "made perfect". Humanity deformed by sin became in him a new humanity, entirely docile to God and completely filled with an astonishing mercy toward his fellow humans.

The contrast with the sacrifices of old is striking. From ritual worship, external and separated from life, to a total personal offering which unfolds in the dramatic events of existence itself. The distinction which was necessary between the Jewish priest and the victim is done away with in the offering of Christ. Christ was at once priest and victim inasmuch as he has offered himself. How was this possible? To this question the author offers, in the densely worded sentence of 9,14, a twofold reply: Christ was able to offer himself because he was worthy of being offered, because he was "without blemish"; and he was capable of offering himself "thanks to the eternal Spirit". In contrast to the priests of old, Jesus was completely exempt from all sin and from all complicity with evil (cf. 4,15); he was "holy, innocent, spotless" (7,26). He could therefore present himself before God without risk of displeasing him. Furthermore, the Holy Spirit with which he was filled (Luke 4,1) made him capable of a generosity which was total. In his intense prayer (Heb 5,7-8) Jesus permitted the Spirit of God to penetrate his human existence through and through, including even his tragic death, and to transform everything into a perfect offering. This aspect of the event has been kept in a prayer of the Mass (immediately before the communion); it recalls that it was "with the power of the Holy Spirit" that by his death Christ gave life to the world.

It is interesting to note in this regard that in the offering of Christ the Holy Spirit played the role attributed to the "fire from heaven" in the sacrifices of old (Lev 9,24; 1 Kgs 18,38; 2 Chr 7,1; 2 Macc 1,22; 2,10). And in fact the true "fire from heaven" can only be the Holy Spirit who alone is capable of bringing about the sacrificial transformation. In order for him to bring about the transformation his action must be welcomed in prayer and generous docility (cf. Heb 5,7-8). The New Eucharistic Prayers have the merit to apply this truth to the Christian life. This is particularly true of the Third Eucharistic Prayer, where we ask "that the Holy Spirit make of us an eternal offering" for the glory of God. Clearly it is by setting us afire with charity in union with Christ that the Holy Spirit transforms us into a sacrifice which rises to God.

f) The offering of Christ to God consisted in an act of love extreme (cf. John 13,1; Heb 2,14-18; 4,15-16). It is not for himself but for us that Christ accepted "to learn by his sufferings obedience". He had no need of this painful transformation; he submitted to it "although being Son" (5,8). Once he accepted it for us he is in a position to communicate it to us. If we cling to him in faith, his blood "will purify our consciences" and will allow us afterwards to "render worship to the living God" (9,14).

Because of this, Christ has become, at the end of his Passion, "mediator of a new covenant" (9,15). Jeremiah, who had foretold the new covenant (Jer 31,31-34; Heb 8,8-12), had not thought to specify in what way it would be established. The author of Hebrews observes that according to the Old Testament (Exod 24,3-8; Heb 9,18-21), a covenant between God and men establishes itself on a bloody sacrifice and that, on the other hand, a new covenant requires a sacrifice of a new type (Heb 8,6). The event of Calvary is presented as the fulfillment of this need (9,15-17) and, at the same time, it allows us to grasp the profound reason why this must be so: sinful man had need of complete recasting of his being, a recasting which could be achieved only through death. But it was necessary that death acquire a positive meaning and serve to establish a new relation between man and God as well as a new solidarity among men. This is precisely what the death of Christ brought about, because it was a perfect personal offering.

Christ's death has brought about in a definitive way that of which the worship of the first covenant could only provide the sketch. The death shortened the distance which separated man from God by elevating the humanity of Christ to the heavenly level and introducing it forever into God's intimacy (9,24-28).

8. A Perfection to be Shared (Hebrews 10,1-18)

In the final section of his long central explanation the author underlines the complete change in situation which results for us from the offering of Christ. He first recalls (10,1-3) that the old Law had no real solution to propose as a remedy for human sinfulness. It was condemned to keep repeating the same useless attempts at mediation. We have already explained why these attempts could not succeed; consisting in the offering of immolated animals, the attempts necessarily remained external to man (10,4) and external to God as well (10,5). In place of this ritual worship Christ generously offers his complete personal obedience to his Father: "Behold, I am come to do your will" (10,9; cf. John 6,38; Luke 22,42). Such an offering is obviously accepted by God for it consists in doing what God wills, and far from being external to man now his whole being is involved, for it begins in the heart and proceeds even to the "offering of the body" (10,10). As a result this offering leads us out of the impasse which had been blocking us. The obstacle of sin no longer bars the way. Christ "has offered a sacrifice for sins" (10,12) and this sacrifice has been efficacious: "We have been made holy by the offering of the body of Jesus Christ" (10,10). Thanks to this perfect offering God has finally been able to fulfill his goal of reestablishing a life-giving communication between himself and us (10,10; cf. 2 Cor 5,18-19).

In a thought-provoking sentence (10,14) the author calls attention here to a new difference between the priesthood of Christ and that of the Jewish high priests. According to the Old Testament, when a descendant of Aaron was ritually "made perfect", i.e., consecrated high priest, his consecration was valid for himself alone. He alone was authorized to enter once a year into the sanctuary (Heb 9,7); no one else was permitted to accompany him but all had to remain outside (Lev 16,17). In the case of Christ, however, the opposite is true: the sacrifice of priestly consecration was valid not only for himself but for all believers. This is the meaning of 10,14. The author, who said in 5,9 that Christ has been "made perfect" (or "consecrated") by his painful offering, affirms in 10,14 that "by one offering Christ has made perfect (or "consecrated") forever those whom he sanctifies". In this way the passive aspect to the Passion

(Christ has been made perfect, has received priesthood) also includes an active: Christ made us perfect, he, communicated the priesthood. The reason for this new aspect is easy to understand: the priestly consecration of Christ was not brought about by a ritual of separation, as in the case of the Jewish high priests, but, on the contrary, by an event where he proved to the extreme his solidarity with us. As a result, the transformation obtained could not be limited to him alone — this would have contradicted the very act which produced it — but of necessity had to include as part of itself a dynamic of sharing.

In this sharing of priestly perfection the author recognizes the fulfillment of the new covenant (10,15-18) which, according to Jeremiah, had to be characterized by God acting in human hearts. The tragic history of the Old Testament had made men aware of both the need for a transformation of hearts and the inability of men to change these evil hearts (Jer 18,11-12). When the heart is evil the best laws are useless. But how is the heart of man to be made true, faithful, and generous, docile to God and open to love of neighbor? God had promised to intervene and "to write his law in hearts" (Jer 31,33; Heb 10,16). In order to understand the depth with which the author of Hebrews understands the fulfillment of this promise, it is necessary to recall here the description of the Calvary event which he gave previously (Heb 5,7-8; 10,5-9). Christ Jesus agreed to submit in his human existence to the necessary transformation. He faced the sufferings which the change entailed. In doing God's will (10,7.9) up to the immolation of his own body (10,10) he learned for us obedience (5,8). From now on, then, a new man exists, formed in perfect obedience: he has the law of God inscribed in the deepest part of his being. A "new heart" exists (Ezek 36,26), completely united to God and to his brothers and sisters. This heart, created for us (cf. Ps 51,12), is open to us. If we remain united to Christ this heart is ours. The prophecy of the new covenant thus takes effect for us: we have the law of God written in our hearts.

9. The Situation of Christians (Hebrews 10,19-25)

Having brought to a conclusion the explanation of the central part (7,1 – 10,18), the author sets about, in 10,19, to spell out the consequences for Christian living. First he describes the religious situation of Christians (10,19-21) and invites them forthwith to accept the consequences wholeheartedly (10,22-25). His sentence spontaneously takes on a tone of triumph, for Christians are from now on in a privileged position: free of the hindrances and anguish which oppressed previous generations, they can go forward in complete assurance on the way which has opened up before them: "we have then, brothers, full assurance for the entrance into the sanctuary..." (10,19).

a) Stupendous news: between Christians and God all barriers are down, separations are a thing of the past! Total contrast with the situation of the Old Testament. All they had known was the system of ritual separations. The author has showed its powerlessness (7,18-19a; 9,8-10; 10,1-4). The sanctification hoped for remained beyond grasp. Between the people and God no real mediation was established. The only real result of this system was the strengthening of separations, as we noted above (p. 65) in presenting the outline:

people | priest | victim | God

With Christ all this changes. His perfect personal offering removes all barriers. Taken away is the separation which existed between the victim offered up and God, for Jesus is a victim "without blemish" who has accepted with complete docility the transforming action of the Spirit of God (9,14; 5,7-8). Taken away is the separation between worship and life: Christ has taken on in his prayer all human affliction and has transformed it into offering (5,7-8). Taken away is the separation between priest and victim: in the sacrifice of Christ priest and victim become one, since Christ "has offered himself" (9,14). Taken away, finally, is the separation between priest and people, for the sacrifice of Christ is an act of complete assimilation to his brothers (2,17), an act which establishes a new solidarity, closer than ever, between him and them (5,9). Christ is a priest who includes the people in his own consecration (10,14). In brief, the cross of Christ (+) establishes sharing, wherever it is found, from people on up to God. Thanks to it the outline is transformed and becomes

people + priest + victim + God.

Here is the reason why we are all now invited to draw near to God (10,22). All believers possess this right which previously was the prerogative of the high priest alone (9,7). They even enjoy a greater privilege still, for it is into the true sanctuary that they are authorized to enter, and not into a human construction (8,5; 9,24). And their right is not limited as was that of the high priest to once each year (9,7), it is always valid.

b) But one point must be made clear: the radical change in the situation is caused by the mediation of Christ and is true only for those men and women who accept this mediation. It would be a mistake to think that a person could draw near to God on his or her own resources and in an individualistic manner.

Entrance into the sanctuary is possible only "in the blood of Jesus" (10,19; cf. 9,12). This entrance is achieved by "the new and living way which he has inaugurated for us" (10,20) and which is nothing else than his glorified humanity (cf. the remarks made above, pp. 66-67, on the "tent"). The entrance is brought about under his leadership, for he is the "high priest" who has authority "over the house of God" (10,21; cf. 3,1-6).

This is why the first basic condition for going forward on the new way is not human effort but faith. The author had set forth this view in the First Part of his sermon (2,1) and he had returned to it insistently during the Second Part (3,7 – 4,14). He had presented the glorified Christ first and foremost as "high priest worthy of faith" (3,1-6; 4,14). Now, after the great central explanation it is again faith which he names first, inviting his listeners to draw near to God "in the fullness of faith" (10,22). It is faith, basically, which makes us cling to Christ the mediator and which thus opens the real possibility of living in communion with God. Speaking of faith, the author alludes to the sacraments which lead to faith's fullness: baptism (10,22) and the eucharistic "blood" and "flesh" of Christ (10,19-20). There are no more rites in the ancient meaning of the word, for the Christian sacraments are closely linked with the personal offering of Christ. It is from it alone that they draw all their worth. They make the offering present and active in the existence of the believers so that this existence is transformed.

Because the mediation of Christ is the only way towards Life, to stray from Christ is an evil without cure. The author has already let this be understood when he commented on Ps 95 (Heb 3,7 – 4,11). He spelled it out with even greater clarity before he began his central explanation (cf. 6,4-6). And he restates it now (10,26-31) in terms which are vigorous indeed. Christ obtained salvation for us through his suffering and through his death. Anyone who makes light of this gift of God by returning deliberately to sin has before him only a "terrible expectation of judgment" (10,27). Faith is not a game. It is the most serious of all commitments.

And also the most fruitful. In order to set forth this positive aspect with all desirable fullness the author dedicates to the subject a long section (11,1-40) in which he goes through the Old

Testament from one end to the other and shows that faith is found at the origin of all that has been of value in the religious history of humanity.

c) To faith the author unites closely hope (10,23), for the message received is not merely the revelation of a truth but also a promise and an invitation. The difficulties of Christian life seem to be obstacles to hope; in reality they allow it to become strengthened in endurance (10,36; 12,1-13). With Jesus as model (12,2-3) Christians are called to let themselves be educated by God through trials and therefore to receive within themselves the divine "holiness" which he seeks to communicate (12,10). Trials then should not be for them an occasion of discouragement but, on the contrary, a motive for a hope which is well warranted.

In fact, endurance amid trials unites Christians in a real way to the sacrifice of Christ. Just as Christ in his Passion learned obedience and did God's will (5,8; 10,5-10), so Christians in their trials submit to the transforming divine action (12,5-11) and do God's will (10,36).

d) The sacrifice of Christ presented another aspect, that of fraternal love for all humans. This aspect must also be found in Christian life (10,24). The author insists on this in the last part of his sermon: "Do not forget, he says, doing good and the sharing of goods, for these are the sacrifices which are pleasing to God" (13,16: cf. 13,1-3).

Christian worship, it is evident, is not marginal to life but is at life's core. It is the Christian transformation of existence, a transformation made possible by union with Christ and inseparable from a continual soaring of thanks towards God (13,14). It comes about in a community of believers, docile to its "leaders" who make present the mediation of Christ, high priest worthy of faith (cf. 13,7) and merciful (cf. 13,17).

Conclusion

The more we meditate on the Epistle to the Hebrews the more we are awestruck by the riches which it offers us. To the question which Christians were asking — the question about priesthood — the author replied with remarkable penetration. His reply is unreservedly positive: Christ is our priest. But the reply is not simplistic. Far from applying to the mystery of Christ the idea of priesthood exactly as it had been understood, he deepened the meaning to the point of completely renewing it. He can then show that Christ not only possesses priesthood but that he is the one and only priest in the full sense of the word, for he is the only one to have opened to men and women the way which leads to God and which unites them among themselves. Instead of a worship necessarily external and inefficacious, marginal as regards life, Christ invites us to make an offering which takes the entire reality of our existence and transforms it profoundly by adhering to God as sons and daughters and by dedicating ourselves to each other as brothers and sisters.

A Structured Translation of the Epistle to the Hebrews

INTRODUCTION

The rather unconventional nature of the present translation makes it advisable to introduce the reader at the very outset to the intended purpose and to the means used to achieve this purpose.

Text and Structure

The important word in the phrase "Structured Translation" is, of course, the first. For the purpose here is not to present a new translation but to place in relief the *literary structure* of the Epistle. The English style is entirely subordinate to this purpose. Hence the reader should not be surprised to find the wording in many places unidiomatic and even awkward. For an idiomatic translation he must look elsewhere.

A systematic study of the Greek text of the Epistle to the Hebrews has led me to the conclusion that the author of the Epistle has structured his work with great care and has made use of fixed literary devices to indicate what he has done. I have discussed my findings at length in *La structure littéraire de l'Épître aux Hébreux*, published by Desclée De Brouwer of Bruges in 1963 in the series "Studia Neotestamentica". To this book the reader desirous of a detailed presentation of the matter is referred. A second edition was published in 1976.

Without entering here into any such discussion I wish simply to give the text of the Epistle in a manner which makes the structure clear to the modern reader. For this purpose I have used typographical devices.

This booklet, then, makes available an initial contact with the results of my detailed study. It is also useful as a companion piece to a reading of this study inasmuch as it gives the frame of reference for each of the particular details examined.

The literary devices used to make known the structure are, as I see them, the following:

1) *announcement of the subject*, a brief formula before each major part which presents the theme to be discussed and its principal divisions (cf. 1,4; 2,17-18; 5,9-10; 10,36-39; 12,13);

2) *inclusion*, the use of the same word or words at the beginning and at the end of the development of a subject. Thus, for example, the formula of 1,5 (the beginning of the paragraph), "for TO WHICH of the ANGELS did he EVER SAY..." is resumed in 1,13 to introduce the end of the paragraph, "TO WHICH of the ANGELS has he EVER SAID...";

3) *hook words*, a word or words in the beginning of a paragraph repeated from the end of the preceding paragraph and thus designed to "hook" the two paragraphs together, e.g., the word a n g e l s of 1,4 (end of the exordium) is repeated in 1,5 (beginning of the First Part); in 1,6 and 1,7 the same word is used for the transition between two subdivisions;

4) *characteristic terms*, terms whose repetition within a section give to it a distinctive physiognomy, e.g., the word "angel" in the First Part (1,5–2,18), the word "faith" in Section A of the Fourth Part (11,1-40);

5) *alternation in the use of literary genres*, the change from one type of discourse to another. In the Epistle to the Hebrews the author passes from the tone of doctrinal exposition to the tone of exhortation, and vice versa; the First Part, for example, is formed from two paragraphs of exposition (1,5-14 and 2,5-18), separated from each other by a paragraph of exhortation (2,1-4);

6) *symmetrical arrangements*, patterns formed from correspondences in many details. Such correspondences can be found in large units; one of the most striking instances is the central section (8,1–9,28), where the six subdivisions mutually correspond, two by two, according to a concentric order (the first with the sixth, the second with the fifth, the third with the fourth).

To make possible a precise presentation of these literary devices it would have been preferable to print the original Greek of the Epistle. But convenience and economy as well as the desire to make the work available to those who do not know Greek have led me to choose a translation instead. This translation does not pretend to do anything but give a reflection of the Greek text. It reproduces the Greek as closely as possible, even the word-order, to the point of doing violence at times to the English language.

Typographical Presentation

Presentation of the text puts simultaneously in relief my evidence and my conclusions. By evidence, I mean the literary devices which make possible the understanding of the work's structure; by conclusions, I mean the structure itself, with all its particulars, extending from the organization of the whole to the individual details of treatment.

The organization of the Epistle as a whole appears from the major divisions. After the verses of the Exordium (1,1-4), the translation is divided into five main *Parts*, labeled as such (First Part, Second Part, etc.). The First and Last Parts have only one section; the intervening Parts have two or more *Sections*. Each Section has its own title which is always taken from the Epistle itself. The Sections are in turn divided into *Paragraphs*, which are if necessary subdivided in turn.

The literary devices on which all this organization is based are indicated as follows:

1. The *announcements of the subject* are noted by the words "ANNOUNCEMENT OF..." alongside the relevant portion of the text, the latter being indented (cf. 1,4; 2,17-18; etc.).

The words in the announcements which point to the subject matter of a Section are accompanied by the letter corresponding to this Section: in 2,17, for example, the (B) which follows "*merciful*" indicates that this word characterizes Section B of the Second Part (4,15 – 5,10); it serves as a title of this Section.

The announcement words which are *resumed* by the author in his treatment are printed in italics and followed by a reference to the pertinent verse; e.g., the formula "*in all things*" of 2,17 is printed in italics and followed by the reference "(4,15)" because the same phrase is found in the latter place. At 4,15 the words "*in all things*" are again printed in italics with the reference to 2,17.

2. The words used for an INCLUSION are printed in small capitals and accompanied by the proper reference; e.g., in reading 1,5, "For TO WHICH... did he EVER SAY (1,13)...", the reader is informed that the words "to which", "ever", "say", are resumed in 1,13 to form an inclusion; at 1,13 he finds the corresponding reference to 1,5.

It is important to note that the inclusions can be multiplied in the same context and fit into each other. For example, the final verse of Chapter 7 contains the termination of three different inclusions: the word HIGH-PRIESTS marks the beginning and end of the small subdivision 7,26-28; the word OATH-TAKING marks the beginning and end of a longer subdivision, 7,20-28; the participle of the verb TO FULFILL corresponds to the noun FULFILLMENT (7,11) and the two thus delimit the large Paragraph 7,11-28.

Inversely, the noun FULFILLMENT serves as the beginning of two inclusions, the one of which ends at 7,19, the other at 7,28, as was just stated. Hence the word in 7,11 is followed by two references, 7,19 and 7,28.

The word ANGELS in 1,5 is used for several inclusions: the subdivision 1,5-6; the Paragraph 1,5-13; the Part 1,5–2,16. For the subdivision, it is the only indication of an inclusion; for the Paragraph, it completes the formula noted above: "To which did he ever say...."; for the Part, it is a member of another formula of inclusion which encloses the last paragraph of the Part: "FOR... NOT ANGELS..." (2,5-16).

3. The terms which play the role of h o o k   w o r d are printed in s p a c e d   t y p e and followed by the relevant reference.

It not infrequently happens that a word which serves as a hook word performs at the same time another function: for example, though the word a n g e l s in 1,4 is only a hook word, in 1,5 the same word is used both as a hook word, joining 1,5 and 1,4, and as the beginning of an inclusion. It is accordingly printed in small, spaced capitals: A N G E L S, the spacing indicating the function of hook word, the small capitals indicating the function of inclusion.

There are other instances of double function. For example, words forming an inclusion also serve as a resumption of an announcement. Such is the case of the word *HIGH-PRIEST* at 3,1, and the word is accordingly printed in italic small capitals. The accompanying references permit the reader to find the explanation without difficulty.

4. *Characteristic words or phrases* and various correspondences in detail are not indicated. The latter are often so numerous that the text would have had to be confusingly complicated to indicate them. This is an aspect of my detailed study of the Epistle which is accordingly available only in the volume in the "Studia Neotestamentica" series.

5. The *alternation of literary genres* has not been indicated by the typography but by the titles of the passages in question.

6. Certain of the *symmetrical arrangements* have been indicated either by the physical arrangement of the text (e.g., in 1,1-2, "spoke" is placed beneath "spoken", "to us" under "to the Fathers", "Son" under "prophets"), or by such expedients as that employed in the Central Section (8,1–9,28), where the same letters indicate the mutually corresponding subdivisions: a and A, b, and B, c and C.

In attempting to be as faithful as possible to the Greek text I have joined by *hyphens* the words of an English phrase which is used to translate one Greek word. For example, the three words "by-varied-stages" (1,1) indicate a translation of one Greek word, πολυμερῶς.

When an English word does not have a material counterpart in the Greek, it is placed in brackets. For example, the phrase "for whom [are] all things" in 2,10 translates δι᾽ ὃν τὰ πάντα.

I would note in closing that the arrangement of the text is in no way intended to indicate rhythm. The arrangement aims only to follow the movement of the thought with particular reference to the structure, in order to make reading as easy as possible.

That is, incidentally, the ultimate aim of all my work: to make reading the Epistle to the Hebrews at once more pleasant and more profitable through a better understanding of the literary structure which unites all the riches of the Epistle into a living whole.

NOTE FOR THE ENGLISH TRANSLATION: For this English version I have indicated several improvements over the French edition. The text of the epistle has been translated from the Greek in accordance with the principles outlined above. Fr. Swetnam has also endeavored to translate a given Greek word or phrase by the same English word or phrase throughout the Epistle. I wish to express my gratitude to Fr. Swetnam for making my work available to an English-speaking audience.

GENERAL OUTLINE
OF THE EPISTLE TO THE HEBREWS

a :		1,1-4	Exordium
I		1,5–2,18	A name so different from the name of the angels
II	A	3,1–4,14	Jesus, high-priest worthy of faith
	B	4,15–5,10	Jesus, compassionate high-priest
III	—	5,11–6,20	Preliminary exhortation
	A	7,1-28	Jesus, high-priest according to the order of Melchizedek
	B	8,1–9,28	Come to fulfillment
	C	10,1-18	Cause of an eternal salvation
	—	10,19-39	Final exhortation
IV	A	11,1-40	The faith of the men of old
	B	12,1-13	The endurance required
V		12,14–13,18	Straight courses
z :		13,20-21	Peroration

EXORDIUM

1,1   By-varied-stages and in-varied-ways in-times-of-old
       God, having-spoken to the Fathers in the prophets,
1,2   with the end of these days
              spoke   to   us   in a   Son,
       whom he established [as] heir of all things,
       him by whom he had made the ages;
1,3   who, being the shining-forth of his glory
              and the imprint of his inner-being,
       and sustaining all things
              with the utterance of his power,
     after-having-effected purification from sins,
     took-his-seat to the right of the majesty on high,
1,4   having become as superior
  ANNOUNCEMENT   to the a n g e l s (1,5)
  OF   as [the] name he has inherited [is]
  THE FIRST PART   so different from them.

FIRST PART

"A name so different from the name of the angels"

FIRST PARAGRAPH: *Son of God*

— **first contrast**

1,5   For TO WHICH of the ANGELS (1,4; 1,6; 1,13; 2,16) DID he
     EVER SAY (1,13):

> My SON (1,5b) are you,
> I today have begotten you;

and again:

> I shall be to him a father
> and he shall be to me a SON (1,5a)?

1,6   Further, when he again brings the first-born into the universe
     he says:

> And may there be prostrate before him
> all ANGELS (1,5; 1,7) of God.

— **second contrast**

1,7   And of the a n g e l s (1,6) he says:
      He who makes his angels SPIRITS (1,14)
      and his cult-MINISTERS (1,14) a flame of fire.
1,8   But of the Son:
      Your throne, God, [is] to the age of the age!
   and:
      The sceptre of equity [is] sceptre of your rule,
1,9   you loved justice and hated lawlessness;
      because of this, God, your God anointed you
      with the oil of triumph above your fellow-sharers;
1,10 and:
      You in the beginning, Lord, established the earth,
      and works of your hands are the heavens;
1,11   they will perish but you will abide;
      and all [of them] will become antiquated like a garment,
1,12   and like a cloak will you fold them away,
      like a garment also will they be replaced,
      but you, you are the same, and your years will not fail.

— **third contrast**

1,13 Further, TO WHICH of the ANGELS has he EVER SAID (1,5):
      Sit at my right
      until I have placed your enemies [as] a footstool of your
      feet?
1,14 Are not all MINISTERing SPIRITS (1,7)
      sent for serving those who-are-about to-inherit salvation?

SECOND PARAGRAPH: *Paraenesis*

2,1   Because of this it-behooves us especially to attend to the things
      heard, lest we ever drift-away.
2,2   For if the word spoken through angels became confirmed
      and every transgression and disobedience received a just
      recompense,
2,3   how shall we escape having neglected such a salvation
      which, having taken a beginning of-being-spoken through the
      Lord,
      was confirmed by the hearers for us,
2,4   with God acting-as-co-witness
      by signs and portents and various marvels-of-power
      and by distributions of holy spirit according-to his will.

THIRD PARAGRAPH: *Brother of men*

— the triumph of a son of man

2,5   FOR NOT to ANGELS (2,16) did he SUBORDINATE (2,8)
       the universe to come about which we are speaking;
2,6   someone has somewhere given witness, saying:

> Who is man, that you are mindful of him?
> or a son of man, that you have care for him?

2,7   You ranked him for a while below the angels,
       with glory and honor you crowned him,
2,8a   everything you subordinated under his feet.

For in the subordinating to him of all things
he left nothing that was to him not-SUBORDINATE (2,5;
2,8b).

2,8b   Now we do not-yet see
       that to him all things have been s u b o r d i n a t e d (2,8a);
2,9   but the one for a while ranked below the angels
       — Jesus — we regard
       because of the suffering of the death
       crowned with glory and honor,
       so that by [the] grace of God he might-have-tasted death for all.

— the solidarity of redemption

2,10   For it was fitting that he for whom [are] all things
                          and through whom [are] all things,
       in leading many sons to glory,
       should give the leader of their salvation fulfillment through
       sufferings.
2,11   For the sanctifier and the sanctified [are] all from one.
       For this reason he is not ashamed to call them brothers,

2,12   saying:

> I will announce your name to my brothers,
> in the midst of assembly will I praise you;

2,13   and again:

> I shall be trusting in him;

and again:

> behold myself and the c h i l d r e n (2,14) whom God
> has given me.

2,14 Because therefore the c h i l d r e n (2,13) have received-in-
common blood and flesh,
he also did likewise share in the same
so that through the death he might-render-powerless
the one holding the control of the death — that is, the devil —
2,15 and that he might-deliver those who by fear of death
through all the life were bound by slavery.
2,16 FOR certainly NOT ANGELS (2,5; 1,5) does-he-take-charge-of,
but [the] seed of Abraham   does-he-take-charge-of.

2,17

ANNOUNCEMENT OF
THE TWO SECTIONS
OF THE SECOND
PART

2,18

Hence *he had* (5,3)
in all things (4,15) *to become-like* (4,15)
his brothers so that he might-become a
merciful (B) (4,16)
and *w o r t h y   o f   f a i t h* (A) (3,2)
h i g h - p r i e s t (3,1; 4,15) *for the things
of God* (5,1) in order to expiate the *sins*
of the *people* (5,3);
for in what he *suffered* (4,15) himself,
having-been-tested (4,15), he *is able* (4,15)
to those-being-tested *to offer-help* (4,16).

SECOND PART

A. FIRST SECTION: Jesus, high-priest worthy of faith

FIRST PARAGRAPH: *Jesus and Moses, worthy of faith*

3,1 Whence, holy brothers, sharers in a HEAVENLY (4,14) calling,
consider the apostle and *HIGH-PRIEST* (2,17; 4,14)
of our PROFESSION — JESUS — (4,14)
3,2 [who is] being *w o r t h y   o f   f a i t h* (2,17) for the one-who-
made him, just as Moses in his entire house.
3,3 For he has been deemed-worthy of more glory than Moses,
as much as has more honor than the house
the one who fashioned it.
3,4 For every house is fashioned by someone,
but the one having-fashioned all things [is] God.
And Moses indeed [is said to be] faithful in his entire house
3,5 as servant,
in witness to the things-to-be-spoken,
3,6 whereas Christ, as Son, over his house;
whose house are we,
if we maintain the accorded-right and the glorying in the hope.

SECOND PARAGRAPH: *warning against lack of faith*

— **quotation**

3,7   Hence, as the Holy Spirit says:
            Today, if you hear his voice,
3,8   do not harden your hearts as in the provocation
            at the day of testing in the desert,
3,9   where your fathers tested in a probing
3,10   and saw my works forty years.
            Hence I became-enraged at that generation
            and said: Always they wander in heart;
            they did not know my ways,
3,11   as I swore in my wrath:
            If they shall enter into my rest!

— **commentary**

3,12   LOOK (3,19), brothers, lest there ever be in anyone of you
        a wicked heart of NON-FAITH (3,19) in the defecting from the
        living God,
3,13   but encourage each other at every day
        as long as the "Today" will be called,
        lest any of you be hardened by the deception of sin.
3,14   For we have become sharers of the Christ
        if the beginning of the inner-assurance we maintain firm
        until the end,
3,15   while it is said:
            Today if you hear his voice,
            do not harden your hearts as in the provocation.
3,16   For who having-heard did-the-provoking?
        [Was it] not all those gone-out of Egypt thanks to Moses?
3,17   Against whom did he become-enraged for forty years?
        [Was it] not against those who sinned,
        whose corpses fell in the desert?
3,18   To whom did he swear that [they] would not enter into his rest
        if not to the unfaithful?
3,19   And we LOOK (3,12) [seeing] that they were not able to
        e n t e r (4,1) because of NON-FAITH (3,12).

4,1   Let us fear therefore lest ever
        — a promise remaining of ENTERING (3,19; 4,5) INTO his
        REST (4,5) —
        anyone of you should be shown to be wanting.

4,2   For we have also received-the-good-news just as they,
but the word of the hearing did not profit them
who had not been fused by the faith with the ones who-
had-heard.
4,3   For we enter into the rest, we who had-faith,
just as he has said:
>As I swore in my wrath:
>If they shall enter into my rest!

the works, indeed, having occurred from the production of the
world.
4,4   For it has been said somewhere about the seventh [day]
thus:
>And God rested on the seventh day from all his works.
4,5   And in this [place] again:
>If they will ENTER (4,1; 4,6) INTO my REST (4,1)!

4,6   Because then it remains that some ENTER (4,5; 4,11) INTO it
and [since] those who had previously received-the-good-news
did not enter because of UNFAITHFULNESS (4,11),
4,7   again he sets a day "today",
saying in David, after so much time,
just as it had been said:
>Today if you hear his voice
>do not harden your hearts.
4,8   For if Jesus [= Josue] had made them rest,
he would not be speaking about another day after these things.
4,9   There remains, therefore, a Sabbath-rest for the people of God.
For he who entered into his rest,
4,10   he also rested from his works just as God from his own.
Let us hasten therefore to ENTER (4,6) INTO that rest
4,11   lest anyone fall in the same model of UNFAITHFULNESS (4,6).

— **praise of the Word**

4,12   For alive [is] the WORD (ΛΟΓΟΣ 4,13) of God and active
and sharper than any two-edged sword and penetrating
into [the] division of soul and spirit, joints and marrow,
and discerning dispositions and thoughts of the heart,
4,13   and there is no creature not visible before him,
but all things [are] bare and laid-open to his eyes,
and [it is] to him [that] for us [is] the RECKONING (ΛΟΓΟΣ
4,12).

4,14 CONCLUSION -   H a v i n g (4,15) therefore a great *HIGH-*
    INCLUSION   *PREST* (3,1; 4,15) who-has-gone-through
                  the HEAVENS (3,1) — JESUS (3,1), the Son of
                  God —
                  let us hold fast to the PROFESSION (3,1).

B. SECOND SECTION: Jesus, compassionate high-priest

— introduction: paraenesis

4,15 For we do not h a v e (4,14) a *HIGH-PRIEST* (2,17; 4,14;
     5,10) *unable* (2,18) to *SUFFER* (2,18; 5,8) with our weaknesses,
     but [one] *tested* (2,18) *in all things* (2,17) in *like-manner* (2,17)
     without sin.
4,16 Let us approach therefore with accorded-right to the throne of
     the grace so that we might receive *mercy* (2,17)
     and find grace for timely *help* (2,18).

— definition of the high-priest

5,1 For every HIGH-PRIEST (5,10) taken from men
    is constituted for men *in regard to the things of God* (2,17),
    so that he might offer gifts and sacrifices for sins,
5,2 able to suffer-with the ignorant and erring
    since he also is surrounded with weakness,
5,3 and because of it he *has* (2,17), just as for the *people* (2,17)
    so also for himself, to offer for *sins* (2,17).
5,4 And not anyone takes for himself the honor,
    but [one] being called by God,
    just as Aaron.

— application to the Christ

5,5 Thus also the Christ:
    [it is] not [he who] glorified himself to become high-priest,
    but the one speaking to him:
        My son are you; I today have begotten you,
5,6 just as in another [place] he says:
        You [are] a priest for the [eternal] age according to the
        order of Melchisedec;
5,7 who, in the days of his flesh, having offered petitions and sup-
    plications
    to the one able to save him from death, with strong cries and tears,
    and having been heard because of his reverence,
5,8 although being Son, learned from the things he SUFFERED
    (4,15) the obedience,

5,9	ANNOUNCEMENT	and *having-been-given-fulfillment* (7,28) (B),
	OF THE THREE	he became for all those who-obey him a
	SECTIONS OF THE	cause of everlasting *salvation* (9,28) (C),
5,10	THIRD PART	proclaimed by God HIGH-PRIEST (5,1; 4,15; 6,20) *according to the order of Melchizedek* (6,20) (A).

THIRD PART

PREAMBLE

FIRST PARAGRAPH: *paraenesis*

— solid teaching and immature Christians

5,11 About which long for us [is] the account and difficult to say
because you have become SLUGGARDS (6,13) in the hearings.

5,12 For although having had to be teachers for the time-being,
again you have need that someone teach you
the elements of the beginning of the oracles of God,
and you have become [ones] having need of milk and not of
solid nourishment;

5,13 for whoever shares milk lacks experience of justice's word, for
he is an infant;

5,14 but of perfect ones is the solid food,
of those who have the senses exercised through the habit
for the discernment of the noble and the evil.

6,1 For this reason, leaving the account of the beginning of the Christ,
let us move on to the perfection, not laying again a foundation
of repentance from dead works and of faith in God,

6,2 of [the] teaching of baptisms and of [the] imposition of
hands,
and of resurrection of bodies and of eternal judgment;

6,3 and this we shall do if God permits.

— a dead-end or hope

6,4 For [it is] impossible
that those once enlightened and having tasted the heavenly gift
and become sharers of a holy spirit

6,5 and having tasted a noble utterance of God and powers of a
coming age

6,6 and having fallen,
[impossible] again to renew to repentance,
crucifying for themselves the Son of God and making-[him]-
an-example.

6,7   For a land having drunk the rain coming over itself many times
and having produced vegetation useful to those for whom it is
cultivated,
accepts a blessing from God;

6,8   but bearing thorns and brambles
[it is] reprobate and near to a curse, whose end [is] burning.

6,9   But we are certain about you, well-beloved,
in regard to the things-better and having-[to-do] with salvation,
even though we speak thus.

6,10 For God [is] not unjust
to forget your work and the charity which you showed for his
name
in having served and [still] serving the holy ones.

6,11 We desire that each of you show the same earnestness
toward the fulfilling of the hope until the end,

6,12 so that you may not become SLUGGARDS (5,11),
but imitators of those who through faith and long-suffering
inherit the p r o m i s e s (6,13).

SECOND PARAGRAPH: *promise and oath*

6,13 For in p r o m i s i n g (6,12) to Abraham, God,
since he had no one greater to swear by, swore by himself,

6,14 saying:

> Yea, blessing I shall bless you and multiplying I shall
> multiply you.

6,15 And having thus been long-suffering, he obtained the promise.

6,16 For men swear by the greater,
and for them in every controversy
a final-decision for confirmation [is] the oath.

6,17 In this [way] God, wishing more abundantly to show to the
heirs of the promise the unchanging-nature of his plan,
pledged with an oath,

6,18 so that through two unchangeable realities, in which [it is]
impossible that God lie, we might have a strong consolation,
[we] who fled to seize the hope lying-at-hand,

6,19 which we have like an anchor of the soul, unslipping and firm
and entering into the interior of the veil,

6,20 where a forerunner for us entered, Jesus,
according to the order of M e l c h i z e d e k (5,10; 7,1) become
high-priest (5,10) for the [eternal] age.

A. FIRST SECTION

"High-Priest according to the order of Melchizedek"

FIRST PARAGRAPH: *Melchizedek (Genesis* 14,18-20)

— **introduction**

7,1   For this MELCHIZEDEK (6,20; 7,10), king of Salem, PRIEST
(7,3) of God the Most High,
who having MET (7,10) Abraham returning from the defeat of
the kings and having blessed him,

7,2   to whom Abraham apportioned a tithe of everything,
first being interpreted king of justice,
then also king of Salem, that is, king of peace,

7,3   without-father, without-mother, without-genealogy,
having neither beginning of days nor end of life,
but having been likened to the Son of God,
remains PRIEST (7,1) in perpetuity.

— **Melchizedek and the Levitic priesthood**

7,4   Now regard how great [is] this [man]
to whom ABRAHAM (7,9) even gave a TITHE (7,9)
from the spoils — the patriarch.

7,5   And those taking the priesthood from the sons of Levi
have a precept to levy-the-tithe on the people according to the
Law,
that is on their brothers, although [these latter] have-come-
forth from the loins of Abraham;

7,6   whereas he, though without-having-a-genealogy from them,
received a tithe from Abraham,

and blessed him who had the promises.

7,7   Now without any controversy, [it is] the inferior [who] is
blessed by the superior.

7,8   And in-the-one-case men who die receive tithes,
whereas in-the-other, [the] one-who-has-been-witnessed-to
that he lives;

7,9   and, so to say, through ABRAHAM (7,4) even Levi, the one re-
ceiving TITHES (7,4)
has been tithed,

7,10   for he was still in the loins of his father
when MELCHIZEDEK MET him (7,1).

SECOND PARAGRAPH: *the two priesthoods (Psalm 110,4)*

— insufficiency of the old priesthood and its replacement

7,11 If therefore there had been FULFILLMENT (7,19; 7,28)
      through the Levitic priesthood
      — for on this the people has-been-given-LAW (7,19; 7,28)
      what need would there still be
      that according to the order of Melchizedek another priest arise
      and not be said according to the order of Aaron?

7,12 For, the priesthood changed,
      of necessity also takes-place a change of law;

7,13 for he about whom these things are said
      has shared in a different tribe, from which no one has attended
      the altar.

7,14 For it is manifest that from Juda
      Our Lord has sprung,
      in regard to which tribe in-the-matter-of priests Moses spoke
      nothing.

7,15 And even more fully manifest is it
      if [it is] according to the likeness of Melchizedek
      [that] another priest arises

7,16 who has become [priest] not according to a law of fleshly
      precept
      but according to a power of indestructible life.

7,17 For witness-is-borne that
          you [are] a priest for the [eternal] age
          according to the order of Melchizedek;

7,18 for removal of a previous precept is-taking-place
      due to its weakness and uselessness

7,19 — for the LAW (7,11) FULFILLED (7,11) nothing —
      whereas an introduction of a better hope [is taking place],
      with which we draw near to God.

— superiority of the new priesthood

7,20 And as far as [it is] not without an OATH-TAKING (7,28) —
for they have become priests without an oath-taking,
7,21 whereas he, with an oath-taking,
through the one saying to him:
    The Lord has-taken-an-oath and will not repent,
    You [are] a priest for the [eternal] age —
7,22 just so far has Jesus become guarantor of a better covenant.

7,23 And they have become priests in-numbers
due to being prevented by death from lasting,
7,24 whereas he, due to his remaining for the [eternal] age,
has the permanent priesthood;
7,25 whence he is able to save to perfection
.those who approach God through him,
always living to intercede for them.

7,26 For such a HIGH-PRIEST also befitted us,
holy, innocent, immaculate,
separated from the sinners and become higher than the
heavens,
7,27 who does not have daily a necessity, as the high-priests,
of offering-up sacrifices previously for his own sins
and then [for] those of the people,
for this he did once-for-all in offering-up himself.
7,28 For the Law constitutes as HIGH-PRIESTS (7,26) men having
weakness,
while the word of the OATH-TAKING (7,20), the [oath-taking]
after the LAW (7,11), [constitutes] a son *come-to-FULFILLMENT*
(7,11; 5,9) for the [eternal] age.

B. CENTRAL SECTION

"Come to fulfillment"

FIRST PARAGRAPH: *inadequacy and replacement of the old worship*

c: the old worship, earthly and figurative

8,1   GENERAL   Now [the] chief point of the things-being-said:
      INTRODUCTION   we have such a high-priest
                       who sat at the right of the throne of the Maj-
8,2   esty in the heavens, CULT-MINISTER (8,6) of the
                       sanctuary and of the true tent, which the Lord
                       set up, not man.

8,3   For every high-priest is constituted to OFFER (9,28) GIFTS AND
      SACRIFICES (9,9), whence the need for him also to have
      something which he might offer.
8,4   If then he were on the earth he would not be even a priest,
      [those] existing who offer the gifts according to the Law,
8,5   who worship at a model and draft of the heavenly things,
      just as was instructed Moses as he was about to accomplish
      [building] the tent:
            For, Look, he says, you are to make everything
            according to the type shown you on the mountain.

8,6   Now [it is] a quite different MINISTRY (8,2) [that] he has obtained,
      in proportion as he is mediator of a better disposition,
      which has been made-law on better promises.

b: the first covenant imperfect and provisional

8,7   For if that FIRST [disposition] (8,13) had been blameless
      there would not have been sought a place for a second.
8,8   For, blaming them, he says:
            Behold days are coming, says [the] Lord,
            and I shall conclude with the house of Israel and with the
            house of Juda a new disposition,
8,9   not according to the disposition which I made with their
            fathers
            on the day of my taking their hand to lead them out of
            the land of Egypt.
            Because they did not abide in my disposition
            I also did not take care of them, says [the] Lord.

8,10   For this is the disposition which I shall dispose for the
house of Israel after those days, says the Lord:
giving my laws into their thoughts and upon their hearts I
shall inscribe them, and I shall be for them God and they
will be for me a people;

8,11   and they will not teach each his fellow-citizen and each
his brother
saying: Know the Lord,
for all will know me, from the small to the great of them,

8,12   because I shall be merciful to their injustices
and of their sins I shall not be mindful more.

8,13 In saying "new" he has made-antiquated THE FIRST (8,7; 9,1).
What [is] becoming antiquated and old [is] near disappearance.

a: the old and powerless institutions of worship

9,1   The first (8,13) also, therefore, had the RITES (9,10) of
WORSHIP (9,6; 9,9) and the sanctuary [which was] of-the-world.

9,2   For a tent was FASHIONED (9,6), the first
— in which [were] the lampstand and the table and the presentation of the breads — which is called * holy;

9,3   and behind the second veil, a tent, the one called * holy among
holies

9,4   having a golden censer and the ark of the disposition covered
all about with gold — in which [was] a golden urn having the
manna and the staff of Aaron that budded and the tables of
the disposition —

9,5   and above it, Cherubim of glory shading the propitiatorium,
about which it is not now [in place] to say in detail.

9,6   With these thus FASHIONED (9,2),
into the first tent, at all [times], enter the priests
accomplishing the WORSHIP (9,1; 9,9).

9,7   but into the second, once a year, only the high-priest,
not without blood, which he offers for himself and the
sins-of-ignorance of the people;

9,8   the Holy Spirit declaring this,
that the way of the sanctuary has not yet been made manifest,
the first tent still having status;

9,9   this [is] a parable for the period at hand, according to which
GIFTS AND SACRIFICES are OFFERED (8,3) [which are] unable
to give-fulfillment according to conscience to the WORSHIPPER
(9,6; 9,1),

9,10 [based] only on food and drinks and different baptisms,
___ RITES (9,1) of flesh in place until [the] period of rectification.

* We place the accent on the iota of the Greek word.

SECOND PARAGRAPH: *the sacrifice of Christ, efficacious and definitive*

A: the new, efficacious institutions

9,11 But CHRIST (9,14; 9,28),
   having-then-come [as] high priest of the good things to come,
   through the greater and more perfect tent,
   not made-with-hands, that is, not of this creation,
9,12 and not through [the] blood of goats and of calves,
   but through his own blood,
   entered once-for-all into the sanctuary,
   having found an eternal redemption.
9,13 For if the blood of goats and bulls and the ashes of a calf,
   sprinkling the defiled,
   sanctifies as regards the purity of the flesh,
9,14 how much more the blood of the CHRIST (9,11),
   who through an eternal spirit offered himself without-blemish
   to God,
   will purify our conscience from dead works
   unto the worship of [the] living God.

B: the new covenant

9,15 And because of this, of a new DISPOSITION (9,17) is he
   mediator,
   so that, death occurring for the deliverance from the transgres-
   sions in the first disposition,
   the called might receive the promise of the eternal heritage.
9,16 For whever [there is] a disposition
   [there is] a NECESSITY (9,23) that death be-brought of the
   one-disposing,
9,17 for a disposition is confirmed in-the-case-of [the] dead,
   since it is never valid when the one-DISPOSING (9,15) is alive.

9,18 Whence neither the first was inaugurated WITHOUT BLOOD
   (9,22);
9,19 for every precept having been spoken ACCORDING TO THE LAW
   (9,22)
   by Moses for all the people,
   taking the blood of the calves and of the goats
   with water and crimson wool and hyssop,
   he sprinkled the book itself and all the people,

9,20 saying:

> This [is] the blood of the disposition which God pre-
> scribed for you.

9,21 And the tent and all the implements of cult
he sprinkled likewise with the blood.

9,22 And in blood almost all things are purified ACCORDING TO THE
LAW (9,19),
and WITHOUT effusion-of-BLOOD (9,18) does not take place remission.

9,23 [There was] a NECESSITY (9,16) therefore, as the models of the
things in the heavens are purified by these [rites],
that so the h e a v e n l y (9,24) things [be] by better sacrifices
than these.

C: the entrance to heaven

9,24 For not into a sanctuary made-by-hands did enter CHRIST
(9,28), an antitype of the true [sanctuary],
but into the h e a v e n (9,23) itself, to appear before the face
of God for us,

9,25 not so that he might offer himself many times,
as the high-priest enters into the sanctuary every year in the
blood of-another,

9,26 for it would have behooved him to suffer many times from the
production of the world,
whereas now, once, in the conclusion of the ages,
for the removal of the sin, through the sacrifice of himself, has
he been made manifest.

9,27

| | And insofar as it remains for men to die once,
and after this a judgment,

CONCLUSION-
9,28 TRANSITION

thus the CHRIST (9,24; 9,11) OFFERED (8,3)
once
for the taking-away of the sins of many,
a second time — without sin —
will be seen to those awaiting him for *s-
alvation* (5,9).

C. THIRD SECTION

"Cause of an eternal salvation"

A: insufficiency of the Law with its repeated sacrifices

10,1 For the Law, having a draft of the good-things about-to-come
and not the image itself of the realities,
EACH YEAR (10,3)
by the same sacrifices which they OFFER (10,10; 10,14; 10,18)
in perpetuity,
is never able to give-fulfillment to those approaching;
10,2 because would they not have ceased being offered
through the [fact that] those worshipping, once purified,
would no more have had a conscience of sins?
10,3 But in these [sacrifices] themselves [there is] remembrance of
s i n s (10,4) EACH YEAR (10,1).

B: replacement of the exterior sacrifices by the sacrifice of Christ

10,4 For [it is] impossible that the blood of bulls and goats
take away s i n s (10,3);
10,5 Hence, entering into the world, he says:
Sacrifice and OFFERING (10,10) you did not will,
but a body you fitted for me;
10,6 holocausts and [sacrifices] concerning sin you did not
take-pleasure in;
10,7 then I said: behold I have arrived,
in a volume of a book it is written concerning me,
to do, O God, your will.
10,8 Saying above that 'sacrifices and offerings and holocausts and
[sacrifices] concerning sin you neither did will
nor took-pleasure in'
which are offered according to Law,
10,9 then he has said: 'Behold I have arrived
to do your will.'
He removes the first to establish the second.
10,10 In this will we have been made-holy
through the OFFERING (10,1.5) of the body of Jesus Christ
once-for-all.

B': replacement of the standing priests by the priest enthroned

10,11 And every priest stands
       each day ministering-the-cult
       and OFFERING (10,14) repeatedly the same sacrifices,
       which are never able to take away sins,
10,12 whereas he, having offered one sacrifice for sins,
       in perpetuity sat at [the] right of God,
10,13 for the remaining [time] awaiting
           until his enemies have been placed [as] a footstool of his
           feet;
10,14 for by one OFFERING (10,11; 10,1)
       he has given-fulfillment in perpetuity
       to those being made-h o l y (10,15).

A': the new covenant suffices from now on without need of sacrifice

10,15 Now, witnessing for us is also the H o l y (10,14) Spirit,
       for after having said:

10,16   This is the disposition which I shall dispose
           for you after those days,
               [the] Lord says:
           giving my laws,
           upon their hearts and upon their thought I shall inscribe
           them,
           and of their sins and of their lawlessness I shall not
10,17   be-mindful more;
10,18 wherever [there is] remission of these
       [there is] no more OFFERING (10,14; 10,10; 10,1) for sin.

FINAL EXHORTATION

A: from exposition to exhortation

10,19 Having therefore, brothers, ACCORDED-RIGHT (10,35) for the
      entrance of the sanctuary in the blood of Jesus,
10,20 the way which he inaugurated for us, fresh and living,
      through the veil, that is, his flesh,
10,21 and a high-priest over the house of God,
10,22 let us approach with a true heart in fullness of faith
      with hearts sprinkled-pure from a wicked conscience,
      and with a body washed by pure water
10,23 let us maintain unmoved the profession of the hope
      — for faithful [is] the one-who-promised —
10,24 and let us consider each-other
      for the stimulation of charity and noble works,
10,25 not deserting our gathering, as [is] a custom for some,
      but encouraging,
      and the more so in proportion as you look at the approach-
      ing Day.

B: prospects which are frightening for sinners

10,26 For if we voluntarily sin,
      after having taken the knowledge of the truth,
      there remains for sins no more sacrifice
10,27 but a TERRIBLE (10,31) expectation of JUDGMENT (10,30)
      and the burning of a fire about to consume the adversaries.
10,28 [If] someone, having removed [the] Law of Moses,
      without pity, on [the word of] two or three witnesses, shall die,
10,29 by how much do you think shall be deemed worthy of a
      worse punishment the one
            having trampled-upon the Son of God
         and having considered as common the blood of the
            disposition, in which he was sanctified.
         and having outraged the spirit of grace?
10,30 For we know the one who said:
         To me [is] vengeance, I shall pay back;
      and again:
         [The] Lord will JUDGE (10,27) his people.
10,31 [It is] TERRIBLE (10,27) to fall into the hands of [the] living
      God.

B': the generosity of times past

10,32 Now recall the previous days
in which, having been illumined,
you endured frequent struggle with sufferings,
10,33 partly made-a-spectacle by insults and tribulations,
partly having made-common-cause with those so treated.
10,34 For you suffered-with those-in-bonds
and the robbery of your possessions you accepted with joy,
knowing that you have a better possession and one that remains.
10,35 Do not throw-off, therefore, your ACCORDED-RIGHT (10,19)
which has a great recompense.

A': announcement of the Fourth Part

10,36 For of *endurance* (12,1) (B) you have need,
so that, having done the will of God,
you might attain the promise,
10,37   for still a little — how little, how little —
the one coming will arrive and will not delay;
10,38   but my just-man will live from *faith* (A)
and if he withdraws, my soul does not take-pleasure in
him.
10,39 We are not for withdrawal unto perishing,
but for f a i t h (11,1) unto [the] acquiring of soul.

FOURTH PART

A. FIRST SECTION: the faith of the men of old

FIRST PARAGRAPH: *definition and first examples*

— **definition**

11,1 FAITH (10,39; 11,7; 11,39) is a title-deed to things-hoped-for,
     an evidence of realities NOT LOOKED-UPON (11,7);
11,2 for in it WERE-WITNESSED-TO (11,39) the men-of-old.
11,3 By faith we understand that the ages have been fitted by an
     utterance of God so that not from things-visible have
     come-about the things-looked-on.

— **sacrifice of Abel**

11,4 By faith Abel offered to God a more-ample sacrifice than
     Cain,
     through which he was witnessed-to to be just,
     God himself witnessing on his gifts,
     and through which, [though] dead, he still speaks.

— **change of Enoch**

11,5 By faith, Enoch was changed so that he did not see death,
     and he was not found because God had changed him,
     for before the change he had been-witnessed-to
     to have-been-agreeable to God,
11,6 and without faith it is impossible to-be-agreeable,
     for it behooves the one approaching God to have-faith
     that he is and that for those seeking him he becomes one-
     who-recompenses.

— **the ark of Noe**

11,7 By faith Noe, instructed concerning the things not yet
     LOOKED-ON (11,1), [after] having reverenced, fashioned an ark
     for salvation of his house, through which he condemned the
     world,
     and of the justice according to FAITH (11,1) he became h e i r
     (11,8).

SECOND PARAGRAPH: *Abraham*

— exile and land of promise

11,8   By faith Abraham, being-called, obeyed [the order] to
       GO OUT (11,22)
       to the place which he was about to take for a h e r i t a g e
       (11,7)
       and he went out not being-cognizant of where he was going.
11,9   By faith he moved-his-dwelling into the land of the promise
       as [a land] of another,
       in tents dwelling with Isaac and Jacob, the co-heirs of the
       same promise;
11,10 for he was awaiting the city having the foundations,
       of which the architect and builder is God.

— the gift of a posterity

11,11 By faith also Sara herself took power for the production of a
       seed even beyond a favorable-period of age,
       because she considered faithful the one who had made-
       the-promise;
11,12 hence also from one-person they became
       — and these from one [who was like a corpse,] dead —
       as the stars of the heavens in multitude
       and as the sand by the shore of the sea which is past-num-
       bering.

— death and quest for the Fatherland

11,13 With faith died all these,
       not having attained the promises,
       but from-a-distance having seen them and saluted,
       and having-professed that they are strangers and wanderers
       on the earth.
11,14 For the-ones saying such-things make-apparent
       that they are in search of a fatherland
11,15 and if they had kept in mind that [country] from which they
       had walked out, they would have had a period to return;
11,16 but [it is] a better [country] which they desire,
       that is, a heavenly [one].
       Hence God is not ashamed to be-called their God;
       for he prepared for them a city.

— **sacrifice and regaining of the posterity**

11,17 By faith Abraham has offered Isaac, being tested,
and he was offering the only-son, he who had received the
promises,
11,18 to whom it had been spoken that
in Isaac will be called your seed,
11,19 having reckoned that even from [the] dead God [is] able to
raise up;
hence he also attained him in parable.

— **deaths and blessings of the patriarchs**

11,20 By faith also concerning the things-about-to-come
Isaac blessed Jacob and Esau;
11,21 by faith Jacob dying blessed each of the sons of Joseph,
and prostrated above the top of his staff;
11,22 by faith Joseph, ending[-his-life],
had-in-mind concerning the GOING-OUT (11,8) of the sons of
Israel
and prescribed concerning his bones.

THIRD PARAGRAPH: *Moses*

— **the treasures of Egypt and the shameful treatment of the Christ**

11,23 By faith Moses when-born was hidden for-three-months by
his parents
because they SAW (11,27) [that] the child [was] attractive
and they DID NOT FEAR the ordinance of THE KING (11,27).
11,24 By faith Moses, become great,
refused to be said to be a son of the daughter of Pharao,
11,25 having chosen to-be-ill-treated-with the people of God
rather than to have a momentary enjoyment of sin,
11,26 having considered a greater wealth than the treasures of
Egypt
the insult of the Christ;
for he was looking-beyond to the recompense.
11,27 By faith he left behind Egypt,
NOT having FEARED the anger of THE KING (11,23);
for as SEEING (11,23) the Unseeable he held-out.

— the freeing of the faithful, the destruction of enemies

11,28 By faith he has made the Passover and the effusion of the blood,
so that the one exterminating the first-born would not touch them.

11,29 By faith they went through the Red Sea as through dry land, taking trial of which the Egyptians were swallowed-up.

11,30 By faith the walls of Jericho fell, having-been-circled for seven days.

11,31 By faith Rahab the harlot did not perish with the unfaithful, having received the spies with peace.

FOURTH PARAGRAPH: *summary view*

— heroes in triumph

11,32 And what more shall I say? For the time will be lacking me to narrate about Gideon, Barak, Samson, Jepthe, David and Samuel and the prophets,

11,33 those who THROUGH FAITH (11,39) overcame kingdoms, worked justice, obtained promises,

11,34 shut mouths of lions, ³⁴extinguished power of fire,
fled mouths of [the] sword, got-power from weakness,
became strong in war, turned the battle-camps of [those] alien;

11,35a women took from r e s u r r e c t i o n (11,35b) their dead.

— heroes in suffering

11,35b But others were tortured, not accepting the deliverance,
so that they might obtain a better r e s u r r e c t i o n (11,35a);

11,36 others took trial of taunts and whips,
still [others], of chains and prison;

11,37 they were stoned, they were cut-up, they were burnt *;
they died by slaughter of sword,
they went-about in clothes-of-sheepskin, in skins of goats,
suffering-want, suffering-tribulation, suffering-affliction,

11,38 of whom the world was not worthy,
wandering in deserts and mountains and caves and the openings of the earth.

---

* A conjecture, the text being uncertain at this point.

— **conclusion**

11,39 And these all, HAVING-BEEN-WITNESSED-TO (11,2; 12,1)
THROUGH THE FAITH (11,33; 11,1),
did not attain the promise,

11,40 God foreseeing concerning u s (12,1) something better,
so that not without u s (12,1) might they be brought-
to-fulfillment.

B. SECOND SECTION: the endurance required

INTRODUCTION: *call to endurance*

12,1 And so w e (11,40) also,
having such a cloud of w i t n e s s e s (11,39) surrounding
u s (11,40),
after throwing off all encumbrance, even the besetting
* burden,
through *endurance* (10,36) let us run-our-COURSE (12,13)
[in] the struggle lying-at-hand for us,

12,2 gazing at the leader and fulfiller of the faith, Jesus,
who, in place of the joy lying-at-hand for him,
endured the cross, having-regarded-with-contempt shame,
and at the right of the throne of God is seated;

12,3 for take-into-consideration the one-who-has-endured
from the sinners against himself such contradiction,
so that you may not grow-weary, being discouraged in your
souls.

DEVELOPMENT: *motives for consolation*

— **correction a mark of sonship**

12,4 Not yet unto blood have you resisted,
struggling against the sin,

12,5 and you have forgotten the consolation
which to you as to SONS (12,8) reasons:
My son, do not make-light-of the discipline of the Lord,
nor be discouraged being by him reproved,

12,6   for whom the Lord loves he disciplines,
he whips every son whom he receives.

---

* According to the conjecture of A. Vaccari, we read απαρτιαν instead of
αμαρτιαν.

12,7 [It is] for discipline [that] you endure,
as [with] sons is God dealing [with] you.
For what is a son whom [his] father does not discipline?

12,8 If you are without discipline, of which all have become sharers,
thereby bastards and not SONS (12,5) are you.

— **on the uses of God's discipline**

12,9 Furthermore, the fathers of our flesh
we had as disciplinarians,
and we took-[it]-as-a-good-TURN (12,13);
shall we not much more be subordinate
to the Father of the spirits
and we shall live?

12,10 For [it was] during a few days
according to [what] seemed [good] to thcm
that they were disciplining,
while he, insofar as useful,
toward the accepting of his sanctity.

12,11 All discipline for the present
does not seem [a matter] of joy but of sorrow;
but later it returns a peaceful (12,14)
fruit of justice for those having been
exercised through it.

12,12
CONCLUSION-
TRANSITION
ANNOUNCEMENT OF
THE FIFTH PART

Hence: the slackened hands and the
paralyzed knees set-straight,
and make the COURSES (12,1) straight for
your feet, so that the lame
will not take-a-bad-TURN (12,9)
but will rather be healed.

FIFTH PART

"Straight courses"

FIRST PARAGRAPH: *an eschatological warning*

— **the forfeiture by Esau for food**

12,14 **(Intro-**   PEACE (13,20) pursue with all,
      duction)   and the sanctification,
                        without which no one will see THE LORD (13,20),
12,15 watching-out lest anyone [be] too-late for the GRACE (12,28) of
      GOD (12,29)
      lest any root of bitterness sprouting up cause-trouble,
      and through it be infected the many,
12,16 lest anyone [be] impure or profane as Esau
      who, in-return-for one bit-of-nourishment
      gave away his rights-as-first-born;
12,17 for you know that afterwards, willing to inherit the blessing,
      he was repudiated,
      for a place for a change-of-heart he did not find,
      although with tears he sought it.

— **the two religious levels**

12,18 For you have not approached
      a fire that is touched and burns,
      and darkness and gloom and storm,
12,19 and a sound of trumpet and the voice of utterances,
      which those having heard begged that a word more not be
      addressed to them.
12,20 For they did not bear the thing bidden:
          If even a beast touch the mountain,
          it shall be stoned!
12,21 And, so terrible was the thing-made-visible, Moses said:
          I am terrorized and trembling.

12,22 But you have approached
      Mount Sion and [the] city of [the] living God, heavenly Jeru-
      salem,
      and myriads of angels in festive-meeting,
12,23 and an assembly of [the] first-born enrolled in the heavens,

and God, a judge of all,
and spirits of just-ones brought-to-fulfillment,

12,24 and a mediator of a new disposition, Jesus,
and blood of a sprinkling s p e a k i n g (12,25) better than
Abel.

— **reasons for greater docility**

12,25 Look that you do not beg-off from the one s p e a k i n g
(12,24),
for if those did not escape
on earth having begged-off from the one-instructing,
much less [shall escape] we who are turning-away the one
from the heavens,

12,26 whose voice rocked the earth then,
but now has promised, saying:
> Yet one-time I shall shake
> not only the earth but also the heaven.

12,27 The "yet one-time" declares
the changing of the things-rocked as of things-made,
so that the things not rocked remain.

12,28 Hence, accepting an unrockable kingdom, let us have GRACE
(12,15),
through which we might worship in-a-way-agreeable to God,
with reverence and fear.

12,29 For our GOD (12,15) is a consuming fire.

SECOND PARAGRAPH: *Christian attitudes*

13,1 Let the friendship-for-the-brethren remain;
do not forget the friendship-for-guests,

13,2 for through it some, unaware, played-host-to angels;

13,3 stay-mindful of those-in-bonds as ones-being-bound-with-
[them],
> of those-in-affliction as also being yourselves in a body.

13,4 Honored [be] marriage among all,
and the marriage-bed, immaculate;
for impure [persons] and adulterers God will judge.

13,5 Without-love-of-money [be] the mode-of-life, sufficient with
the things present, for he himself has said:
> No, I shall not desert you, nor shall I abandon you!

13,6 So that courageously we may say:
> The Lord for me a helper, I shall not fear;
> what will do to me a human being?

THIRD PARAGRAPH: *dietary observances and authentic Christian fidelity*

13,7   Keep-mindful of your LEADERS (13,17),
       who spoke to you the word of God;
       in contemplating the outcome of their CONDUCT (13,18), imi-
       tate their faith.

13,8   Jesus Christ yesterday and today the same, and for the ages.
13,9   By doctrines various and strange do not be carried-away;
       for [it is] noble [that] by grace be strengthened the heart,
       not by foods
       in which did not profit those [so] proceeding.
13,10 We have a sacrifice-altar
       from which do not have a right to eat
       those worshipping at the tent;
13,11 for the animals of which the blood
       is brought for sin into the sanctuary through the high-priest,
       their bodies are burned-up outside the camp.
13,12 Hence also Jesus,
       that he might sanctify through his own blood the people,
       suffered outside the gate;
13,13 therefore let us go out to him outside the camp in bearing his
       insult,
13,14 for we do not have here a city to-remain,
       but the [one] about-to-come [is what] we search for.
13,15 Through him therefore let us offer-up a sacrifice of praise
       through all [time] to God,
       that is, fruit of lips professing his name.
13,16 And the well-doing and the common-[sharing] do not forget;
       for to such sacrifices is God agreeable.

13,17 Obey your LEADERS (13,7) and be-submissive,
       for they are vigilant for your souls as ones-about-to-return
       account,
       so that with joy they may do this
       and not with sighs, for this [would] not [be] useful for you.
13,18 Pray for us,
       for we are certain that we have a noble conscience,
       in all-things willing nobly to CONDUCT-ourselves. (13,7).

13,19 (**A Word in Parting**)   Abundantly I beg [you] to do this,
                                       so that quite-quickly will I be restored
                                       to you.

PERORATION

13,20   May the God of the PEACE (12,14)

     who led-up from [the] dead
     the shepherd of the sheep, the great,
     in blood of an eternal disposition,
     our LORD (12,14), Jesus,

13,21   fit you in all good
     for the doing of his will,
   doing in you the agreeable before him
     through Jesus Christ,

  to whom the glory for the ages of the ages.

       AMEN.

A Word in Parting

13,22 I beg you, brothers: sustain the speech of the exhortation;
   for with a few [words] I send [it to] you.

13,23 Know that our brother Timothy is released,
   with whom, if he comes quite-quickly, I shall see you.

13,24 Salute all your leaders and all the holy-ones.
   Those from Italy salute you.

13,25   The grace [be] with all of you. Amen.

Abbreviations of Books of Sacred Scripture

Gen	Genesis		Amos	Amos
Exod	Exodus		Obad	Obadiah
Lev	Leviticus		Jonah	Jonah
Num	Numbers		Mic	Micah
Deut	Deuteronomy		Nah	Nahum
Josh	Joshua		Hab	Habakkuk
Judg	Judges		Zeph	Zephaniah
Ru	Ruth		Hag	Haggai
1–2 Sam	1–2 Samuel		Zech	Zechariah
1–2 Kgs	1–2 Kings		Mal	Malachi
1–2 Chr	1–2 Chronicles		1–2 Macc	1–2 Maccabees
Ezra	Ezra			———
Neh	Nehemiah		Matt	Matthew
Tob	Tobit		Mark	Mark
Jdt	Judith		Luke	Luke
Esth	Esther		John	John
Job	Job		Acts	Acts of the Apostles
Ps	Psalm			
Prov	Proverbs		Rom	Romans
Qoh	Qoheleth [Ecclesiastes]		1–2 Cor	1–2 Corinthians
			Gal	Galatians
Cant	Canticle of Canticles [Song of Songs]		Eph	Ephesians
			Phil	Philippians
			Col	Colossians
Wis	Wisdom		1–2 Thes	1–2 Thessalonians
Sir	Sirach [Ecclesiasticus]		1–2 Tim	1–2 Timothy
			Titus	Titus
Isa	Isaiah		Phlm	Philemon
Jer	Jeremiah		Heb	Hebrews
Lam	Lamentations		Jas	James
Bar	Baruch		1–2 Pet	1–2 Peter
Ezek	Ezekiel		1–3 John	1–3 John
Dan	Daniel		Jude	Jude
Hos	Hosea		Apoc	Apocalypse [Revelation]
Joel	Joel			

Index of Scripture Texts

4,36	4
5,30	47
6,5	5
7,48	64
8	5
9,9	64
9,27	4
11,22-30	4
13–15	4
13,33	46, 47
14,13	7
15,22	4
15,40 – 18,5	4
17,24	64
18	5
18,24-28	5
20,7	45
20,7-8	45
21,8	5
21,27-31	11

ROMANS

1,4	46
1,18-32	9
1,21	9
3,1	62
4,14-15	4
5,6-8	13
5,19	4
5,20	4
6,9	62
8,3	4
8,25	31
10,24-25	31
16,3-5	5

1 CORINTHIANS

1,12	5
2,1	32
2,4	32
2,13	32
3,4-6	5
3,22	5
5,7	16
7,7	32
10,14-22	16
11,20	16, 45
11,25	16
14,26	45

15,3	13
15,3-4	47
15,25	4, 47
15,25-27	48
15,27	4
16,2	5

2 CORINTHIANS

1,19	4
5,18-19	69
10,10	32
11	3
11,6	32

GALATIANS

1,1	3
1,2	1
1,12	3
2	4
2,16-21	4
2,20	4, 17
3,1	1
3,13	13
3,19-25	4

EPHESIANS

1,20-21	48
1,20-22	48
1,21	4(2 ×)
1,22	4
2,21-22	52
5,2	4,17
5,25	4

PHILIPPIANS

2,8	4
2,9	4
3,10	47
4,3	4

COLOSSIANS

1,15-17	4
1,16	48
2,10	48
2,15	4, 48
4,18	4